THE UNOFFICIAL

Millennium
Companion

THE COVERT CASEBOOK
OF THE
MILLENNIUM GROUP

VOLUME TWO

THE UNOFFICIAL
Millennium
Companion

THE COVERT CASEBOOK
OF THE
MILLENNIUM GROUP

VOLUME TWO

N. E. Genge

Century · London

Published by Century in 1997

1 3 5 7 9 10 8 6 4 2

Copyright © N. E. Genge 1997

First published in the United Kingdom in 1997
by Century Limited
Random House, 20 Vauxhall Bridge Road,
London SW1V 2SA

Random House, Australia (Pty) Limited
20 Alfred Street, Milsons Point,
Sydney, New South Wales 2061, Australia

Random House New Zealand Limited
18 Poland Road, Glenfield, Auckland 10, New Zealand

Random House, South Africa (Pty) Limited
Endulini, 5a Jubilee Road, Parktown 2193, South Africa

Random House UK Limited Reg. No. 954009

A CIP catalogue record for this book is available
from the British Library

Papers used by Random House UK Limited are natural, recyclable products made from wood grown in sustainable forests. The manufacturing processes conform to the environmental regulations of the country of origin

ISBN 0 7126 78697

Typeset in Officina Sans and Concorde

Design & page make-up by Roger Walker

Printed and bound in the United Kingdom by
Butler & Tanner Ltd, Frome

For Peter

ACKNOWLEDGEMENTS

When I first took on this project, I knew I had a lot to learn in a very short time. I couldn't have done it without the able assistance and steady support of dozens of absolutely wonderful people. It gives me so much pleasure to thank:

Penda MacIntyre, Dean Cant, James Penner, Mark Penner and Ivan Reid, the Group who explains The Group, and the Society of Former Special Agents of the Federal Bureau of Investigation for taking the time from their hectic schedules to illuminate the darker recesses of the human mind, and for leading me through the mass of private consultancy, its limitations and its freedoms.

Walter, Roy, Elaine, Colin, James, Frank, Paul and George, for their consistent support of all the unusual projects in which I entangle them. You all give new meaning to the term 'special' Agents.

Jean, Rebecca, Gloria, Philip and Kazha, for providing transcripts, court records, psychological profiles and forty-three feet of articles and reference books, all in less than four months. We'd never have made it without you.

John Sainsbury, who, in addition to organizing, cross-referencing and filing those forty-three feet of research material, significantly increased the size of that stack by tracking down all the elusive footnotes that make the whole come together. Thank you!

Maria Rejt and Kate Elton at Century for their understanding and patience when this book's production schedule and real life came into conflict – and for allowing me to deal with the important things first. You've no idea how grateful I am for your grace and generosity of spirit.

Ling Lucas, my friend and my agent, for knowing when to be one and when to be the other, for making a very difficult time almost bearable. Thank you, thank you, thank you. And to Ellen van Wees, who keeps us both going in the right direction.

And, to my family, who provide me with more love, joy and support than I could ever deserve. You constantly amaze me.

Contents

Introduction

Though it wasn't so very long ago that I sat down to write the Introduction to Volume I of this series, it's impossible not to realize that all the changes being alluded to early in the season have now come to full fruition.

When the series opened, creator Chris Carter was stressing that this wouldn't be another version of *The X-Files*, and that while Frank Black possessed some unique insights, he wasn't some psychic or supernatural being who could forego all the usual investigative steps other mere mortal detectives seemed to need. For the first half of the opening season, it even seemed that he intended to stick to the stated agenda. Then, word came that some 're-tooling' was in order, that there would be changes, and fans who'd by that time developed some serious interest in Frank Black, his semi-mysterious partners, and the thin line he walked between understanding the madness and succumbing to it, weren't at all sure they liked this new scheme.

Instead of serial killers who followed the basic motive patterns, commonplace notions of greed, lust, or revenge, Frank Black suddenly faced a multitude of enemies – all of whom seemed to know more about him than coincidence, or even really obsessive investigation, should have revealed. The totally human, and therefore remarkably terrifying, killers from episodes like 'Dead Letters' and 'Kingdom Come', almost completely disappeared as the season progressed. No longer were Frank Black and the others actually catching the bad guys; now, they were struggling to make connections between such apparent disparate suspects as Al Pepper and Lucy Butler, trying to understand how Martin, who killed with seeming randomness on one coast, could possibly have been involved, as he claimed, in the murder of Robert Bletcher on the opposite shoreline. The rather vague and general notion that 'something' was behind the sudden upsurge in violent crime had crystallized rather quickly into a single, conspiratorial, enemy.

On the home front, the idea of an inheritable, if wild, talent, something barely hinted at in the first part of the season, wasn't only openly discussed, it became the defacto reason behind at least one episode, 'Sacrament'.

The Black family grew, and was immediately subjected to the same sort of predation that had earned Chris Carter a slew of the 'red shirt' jokes, references to *Star Trek* characters who appeared for the sole reason of dying in the place of one of the regular cast, that already dogged *The X-Files*. With the deaths of Robert Bletcher and, in particular Mike Atkins, it seemed that Carter was following an all-too-familiar path. How long would it be before those early promises would be lost in the suddenly shifting terrain in the *Millennium* universe?

Still, while the changes have undoubtedly been put into practice on-screen, the changing focus hasn't resulted in a wholesale abandonment of the program by its fans.

That's due in large part to the deft handling of storylines. The possibility for such turns in the plotlines was present even in the very first episode. Frank Black's opponents, at least for the present, act in basically human form, even if their 'inspiration' is otherworldly. Black still has someone, as opposed to something, to chase down. And, though the Millennium Group itself failed to produce the new members audiences had been anticipating – and killed off a member whose return we'd been anxiously awaiting! – the present characters, especially that of Peter Watts, continue showing us a depth that keeps us interested. We'll await the return of actresses like CCH Pounder and Lindsay Crouse to keep us intrigued next year.

Overall, though the program's focus has veered sharply from what we were led to expect, *Millennium*'s real essence, Frank Black, remains what he has always been, passionate, persuasive, and driven – regardless of his ultimate goal. As long as this character continues to grow, along with those who surround him, *Millennium* will continue to attract viewers, continue to be exceptional TV.

THE UNOFFICIAL

Millennium
Companion

THE COVERT CASEBOOK
OF THE
MILLENNIUM GROUP

VOLUME TWO

CASE FILE: 'Force Majeure'

CASE SYNOPSIS:

Identical women are committing horrendous acts of suicide, freakish 'natural' disasters provide a stunning backdrop, and a man named Dennis Hoffman is not only claiming to be a member of the Millennium Group, but to know what's happening – and what is yet to come.

KEY CITATION:

'Seven planets align.
Seven people survive with Noah.
Seven different prophecies by Nostradamus
predicting the Apocalypse in May.
Listen! This is the beginning of the
thousand days!'

DENNIS HOFFMAN,
MILLENNIUM GROUP WANNA-BE

VITAL STATISTICS:

Original US Airdate:	02/07/97
Production Number:	4C12
Written by:	Chip Johannessen
Directed by:	Winrich Kolbe

Guest Cast:

Terry O'Quinn	Peter Watts
CCH Pounder	Cheryl Andrews
Brad Dourif	Dennis Hoffman
Kristi Angus	Lauren / Carlin
Sarah Strange	Maura
Morgan Woodward	Iron Lung Man
Cindy Girling	Myra
Timothy Webber	Sheriff Camden
Merrilyn Gann	Carlin's Mother
Carolyn Tweedle	Lauren's Mother
Peter Hanlon	Manager
Mitch Kosterman	Lieutenant
Phillip Mitchell	Uniform #1

Death Toll:	2 women, suicide by immolation and drowning

CASE HISTORY:

5 MAY, 2000: A ONCE IN AN EON SHOW FEATURING A COSMIC LINE-UP Dennis Hoffman

was very sure of his future – and of ours.

'On 5 May, 2000, seven inner planets align for the first time since the great flood. Uranus at the meridian of its epi-center. Earth the focus of the biggest gravitational tug-of-war since the great flood. Catastrophic earth changes on align-ment day. Preceded by abnormal weather patterns now as stresses build.'

Finally turning back to the apocalyptic promise inherent in the show's title, 'Force Majeure' tackles perhaps the most plausible, if literally earth-shattering, of millennial prophe-cies. The planetary alignment of 5 May, 2000, the event that proved such a fixation for not only the Iron Lung Man, the modern-day Noah of the episode, but pseudo-Millennium Group member, Dennis Hoffman, also garners attention from considerably more 'reliable' sources.

In some highly acclaimed science journals, an eminent geophysicist named Dr Tomaschek reported some trends revealed in his earthquake studies that, if proven, have dis-turbing implications. His focus, the 'super-shakers', quakes of more than seven-and-a-half on the Richter Scale, didn't follow any schedule relative to our yearly calendar, but, when he looked at the 130-plus big quakes of the last 40 years, he found a scientifically significant number of them

CAN YOU IMAGINE THE PROP DEPARTMENT'S COLLECTIVE EXPRESSION ON READING, 'NEXT TO AN IRON LUNG...' – THEY WANT WHAT?!

occurred when Uranus lined up near the epicenter of the quakes.

If his study is sound, the results of conjunctions between Uranus and volatile seismic faults may prove routinely devastating. 1923, Tokyo is, by all practical definitions, leveled. 1933, Honshu – for the second time in a decade, Japan faces disaster on an island-wide scale, millions of dollars in damage and hundreds of deaths. In India, in 1950, the Assam quake kills thousands more and, under Uranus's influence, weighs in as one of the strongest quakes in recorded history.

On 5 May, 2000, Uranus will be only one of several planets set to play its part in a cosmic tug-of-war featuring Earth as a relatively delicate sphere perched between some gigantic neighbors. On one side of the equation: a new Moon, the Sun, Jupiter, and Saturn align. On the other side, the rest of the solar system, ranging on the Sun's far side, will then combine to create unique gravitational forces whose consequences have yet to be completely calculated.

Optimists point out that the planets have been floating about in their assigned orbits for a very long time indeed, and that Earth is still spinning through its paces very happily, thank you. True enough. Of course, the last such alignment did just happen to fall in the time period when classical literature refers to the fall of Atlantis 'amid earthquakes shaking the world's roots and the stars in their courses' accompanied by 'seasons of flame' as volcanic eruptions continued the damage.

If vague references from Literature 101 don't convince audiences that something's up, science, that most acceptable of modern religions, is offering up some comments of its own, from a variety of disciplines, all suggesting that while the Earth is still twisting to its own groove, its present face is far different from previous ones. They believe 5 May, 2000, will be the culmination of a series of quakes, volcanic eruptions, and other geothermic activity leading to a terra-forming facelift, a shift of the Earth's very magnetic poles!

Almost needless to say, is that such an event would, in most informed opinions, precipitate mass extinctions of hundreds of species – humanity included.

And how would such a cataclysm come to pass?

Well, geologists have long likened our planet to a series of solid, geologic 'plates' floating around a magma sphere and the analogy is essentially correct. These plates float about, bumping into one another, causing earthquakes that, while nothing more than tremors on a planet-wide scale, have rather significant impacts on local ecosystems. The edge-to-edge grinding of these plates, along with the usual side-effects of volcanic eruptions and tsunami, are indicative of the relative instability of our geologic flotsam. That the Earth's spin isn't exactly uniform is also well known. Put bluntly, we 'wobble'. Even more bluntly, we've become more wobbly as time has passed. Several factors have been put forward to explain the origin of our erratic gyrations, among them the fact that the sheer mass of the Himalayas creates a 'shadow pole', a third point that drags the planet aside as it turns. Unfortunately for the theorists, however, the Himalayas aren't changing fast enough to account for the increasing wobble of our axis.

> **BLOOPER!** As if the storm that opens this episode wasn't weird enough in its own right, the 'hail' hammering the students was made of square ice chunks!

Environmentalists, scientists for whom the Greenhouse Effect is both a question or an answer, think they may have a further explanation for our wobbly trip around our pole. They believe it's the poles themselves that are changing. The cyclical nature of Ice Ages has been suspected for some time, without a strong explanation for the regular encroachment and retreat of the polar ice sheets. One man, Edgar Scenza, has postulated that, as time passes and the ice over the poles thickens effectively moving the surface of each pole as much as four miles above its youthful starting point, the axis is elongated and the 'Himalaya Effect' accentuated. He speculates that, if the wobble overbalances the axis enough, the plates simply slide, altogether, to accommodate the stresses on them. The polar ice, now considerably closer to the unchanging equator, melts and the process starts all over again. A cycle that could explain not only the rhythm of the Ice Ages, but why excavations of areas currently close to the poles frequently reveal the fossilized remains of ecosystems that are obviously equatorial in content.

If these are indeed the factors that could lead to a polar shift, then the Earth is at an interesting point in the cycle. The polar ice is building quickly, currently approaching the four-mile thick point suggested as a critical mass for such a shift while the Earth continues its wobble. The frequency and severity of earthquakes and volcanic eruptions is higher now than at any time in our recorded history, indicating that considerable plate action is already occurring. How will this delicate balance be affected by a planetary alignment that seems pre-destined to exert as much additional stress on our little globe as possible?

Frankly, no one really knows.

A wide collection of prophets have, however, put forth a disconcertingly similar answer to that very question.

CATCH IT? Lauren Padilla supposedly suffered from fourth degree burns to significant parts of her body, including her extremities, yet those beautiful blue eyes were completely untouched? Chances of that happening? Zip. Nada. Zilch.

Nostradamus, who seems to have had his eye on every possible future event, wrote: 'An earthquake will be reported from the base of Asia when Mars, Mercury and Moon align.' Those planets will indeed align during the 5 May, 2000 event. The sceptical may wonder why this conjunction, which must have happened hundreds of times in the past, should suddenly take on significance in 2000. Perhaps it's because when those heavenly bodies were last in alignment, during October 1993, 30,000 people died in a quake in India. And Nostradamus never said his predictions were one-shot affairs...

Still, it's really too early to panic. In fact, if you were to give serious attention to all that's been written on the conjunction, you mightn't have time to get it all in before 5 May, 2000!

Relying on the most prosaic of sciences, mathematics, to calculate the individual effect of each separate planet, John Mosley, writing in *Sceptic* magazine, concludes that, 'If all the planets were to align perfectly, their gravity would raise the ocean tides by one twenty-fifth of one millimeter.' Pointing out the distances involved, he adds, 'A book you hold in your hands exerts a billion times as much tidal force as the planet Mars when Mars is at its closest.'

Writing in another branch of pure mathematics, chaos theory, Martin Crittenly managed to come up with a com-

TESTIMONY TRIVIA 13

QUESTIONS

Easy stuff – one point for each correct answer.

1 What was Lauren reading on campus just before she died?
2 Lauren turned down an appointment at which university?
3 What did Cheryl Andrews find carved into Lauren and Carlin's arm?
4 How did Peter Watts describe the position of the dead girls' hands?
5 What type of drugs were both girls self-injecting?

Tough stuff – take two points for every correct response.

6 What institute did both Lauren and Maura attend?
7 What number did Frank Black use to reach Peter Watts?
8 What was the number of Dennis Hoffman's efficiency apartment?
9 Where did Dennis Hoffman plan to be on 5 May, 2000?
10 Name Jordan's new school.

pletely contradictory conclusion. According to chaos theory, any change, even a minute change, makes a significant difference to interconnected systems. Chaos theory postulates the link between a drop of rain falling in Arizona and a breeze tickling some Tuscan grapes – and the theory is surprisingly sound, at least theoretically. And the connections between planets, sunspots and tides are already proven to be much tighter than those between puddles and wine. Chaos theorists watch the magnetic pole drift ever farther from the geographic pole and wonder what other connections the 5 May, 2000 alignment may reveal.

Relatively new fields like quantum theory reinforce the notion that two seemingly disparate events could actually be related, not necessarily as a cause-effect relationship, but as two inevitable outcomes of a singular event. Maybe that's what the 'mutant smart' Lauren discovered in her study of esoteric mathematics.

One thing is already certain. Several areas well known to be practically immune to natural disasters, all some distance from any coastline, all over 2000 feet in elevation, are already reporting an upsurge in tourism bookings for 5 May, 2000.

NOTEBOOK:

For Peace...

Catherine's reference to Buddhist monks immolating themselves in protest of the Vietnam 'conflict' probably evoked powerful images for those old enough to remember the death of the Venerable Thich Quang Duc. Though he was not the first – or the last – of the monks to protest the American backing of South Vietnam's Diem regime, he was the first to set himself ablaze in front of scores of his followers and, perhaps more importantly, in front of dozens of international journalists. Headlines on 11 June, 1963, screamed out the horror of one man's death. It was, for many, a singular moment when politics, propaganda, hype, and heresy ceased to exist. Vietnam, its struggles and its misery, became real in a new, deeply disturbing way.

Though Vietnam's political landscape has changed considerably in the 35 years since Thich Quang Duc's death, the peace he so desperately sought, religious freedom and political stability continue to be precious commodities all-too-easily lost.

Dozens of other Buddhist monks, many well into their seventies and eighties, still protesting the North Vietnamese government's oppression of anything other than the state-approved version of Buddhism, were confined to forced labor camps as recently as 1995, despite local protests and international pressure.

On 15 April, 1995, Sabine Kratze, a German student of Vietnamese culture and Buddhism, followed in Thich Quang Duc's footsteps and ended her life by ritual self-immolation to draw international attention to the plight of the Unified Buddhist Church of Vietnam.

A N S W E R S

1   Greever's 'theory and example of Point-Set Topology'
2   Oxford
3   The astrological symbol for 'conjunction'
4   The Mandala Position
5   Fertility drugs
6   Washington Polytechnic University
7   555-0172
8   Lucky number 7
9   A motel in Pocatello, Idaho
10 Green Valley Day School

YOUR SCORE:

INCIDENTALS:

Did the film footage of the floods look oddly familiar? The images were taken from real news coverage of floods that devastated the Saguenay River Valley in southern Quebec. That single house sitting amid the torrents of water was one of only three to survive in that area.

☐

Yes, Virginia, there really is a Pocatello, Idaho. It's just east of the American Falls Reservoir and just west of Soda Springs, smack dab in the Snake River Plain.

☐

FILMOGRAPHY:

BRAD DOURIF

Some actors possess the uncanny ability to so enthrall an audience with their present performance that viewers completely forget the actor ever appeared in any other role. It's

IN THIS CORNER, THE GROUP; IN THIS CORNER, THE GROUPIE

only after the performance that impressions of other occasions, other characters, other scenarios begin to seep back into the audience's consciousness. Brad Dourif is just such an actor, and the list of credits to contemplate after watching his completely convincing appearance in 'Force Majeure' is suitably broad and impressive.

Alien 4 (1997) – Dr Gediman
Nightwatch (1997)
Black Out (1996)
Escape to Witch Mountain (1995)
Murder in the First (1995) – Bryon Stamphill
Phoenix (1995) – Reiger
'Babylon 5' Passing Through Gethsemane (1995)
– Brother Edward
Color of Night (1994) – Clark
Death Machine (1994) – Jack Dante
Escape from Terror:The Teresa Stamper Story (1994)
– Sheriff Douglas
Wild Palms (1994) – Chickie Levitt
'The X-Files' Beyond The Sea (1994) – Luther Lee Boggs
Amos and Andrew (1993) – Officer Donaldson
Trauma (1992) – Dr Lloyd
Dead Certain (1992) – John Barnes
Final Judgement (1992) – Father Tyrone
Body Parts (1991) – Remo Lacey
Critters 4 (1991) – Al Bert
Jungle Fever (1991) – Leslie
London Kills Me (1991) – Hemingway
Common Bonds (1990) – Johnny Reynolds
Exorcist III: The Legion (1990) – The Gemini Killer
Stephen King's Graveyard Shift (1990) – The Exterminator
The Horseplayer (1990) – Bud Cowan
Desperado: The Outlaw Wars (1989) – Camillus Fly
Spontaneous Combustion (1989) – Sam
Terror on Highway 91 (1989) – Keith Evans
Mississippi Burning (1988) – Deputy Clinton Pell

Fatal Beauty (1987) – Leo Nova
Blue Velvet (1986) – Raymond
Rage of Angels: The Story Continues (1986)
– Seymour Bourne
Dune (1984) – Pieter De Vries
Heaven's Gate (1980) – Mr Eggleston
Wise Blood (1979) – Hazel Motes
Eyes of Laura Mars (1978) – Tommy Ludlow
One Flew Over the Cuckoo's Nest (1975) – Billy Bibbit

Brad Dourif also portrayed Charles Lee Ray in the 1988 film *Child's Play* before continuing as Chucky's Voice for the remainder of that film and its two sequels (1990, 1992).

LANCE HENRIKSEN IN 'ALIEN'

SUCH DRIVE, SUCH PASSION, BUT WHERE WILL IT LEAD?

CASE FILE: 'The Thin White Line'

CASE SYNOPSIS:

When Frank Black witnesses the death of a young woman with wounds identical to those inflicted by a serial killer he knows is still in a maximum security facility, he's quickly drawn into the search for a copycat killer. The investigation is made all the more difficult by Frank's own unresolved guilt and the looming necessity for him to once more interview the original killer, a man who murdered Frank's colleagues and left Frank marked for life.

KEY CITATION:

'Look, you ever share your life so completely
with another human being that you ... you – you
eat, you sleep, you breathe everything the same?!
I touched his life like no one else can
'cos I was in here with him! I mattered,
and he mattered. I lived as Jacob
and he lived as me!'

RICHARD HANCE

VITAL STATISTICS:

Original US Airdate: 02/14/97

Production Number: 4C13

    Written by: Glen Morgan and James Wong

    Directed by: Thomas J Wright

Guest Cast:

Jeremy Roberts	Richard Hance
Scott Heindl	Jacob Tyler
Eric Breker	Howard Rothenburg
Nancy Sivak	Anne Rothenburg
Larry Musser	The Warden
Tom Heaton	Store Clerk, Sam
Allan Harvey	Agent Johnson
Ken Tremblett	Agent Riley
Mark Holden	Agent Clark

Death Toll: 1 woman, stabbed to death

               1 man, shot

               1 woman, unknown means

               1 man, unknown means

               7 flashback victims, 1 woman

CASE HISTORY:

RELATIONSHIPS BEHIND THE WALLS

'I've been questioning myself, my actions. We think we're doing our job, putting these guys away. All we do is put them in jails and prisons, we're hiding them from sight.'

The world behind prison bars as depicted in hundreds of films wouldn't encourage viewers to really think of the lives slowly being played out there. Most films that involve prisons, especially in recent years, have focused on two issues. The first is, naturally enough, escape. *The Great Escape*, *Papillion*, and *Escape From Alcatraz* are classics in the genre. *Fortress* put a futuristic spin on the old story. *The Shawshank Redemption* was a quieter, more dramatic film, but an escape film nonetheless and the prison portrayed wouldn't even be recognizable to modern convicts. *The Rock* had its own twist when it made the lead character break back into Alcatraz having already escaped it once!

The second rash of prison flicks, copycats in many ways, have been the Death Row pictures. *Dead Man Walking* received both popular and critical praise. Sharon Stone's *Last Dance* certainly took the story into new areas, but it was still a Row flick. Grisham's *The Chamber* told us almost everything anyone would want to know about last-ditch appeals, and hinted at the fact that, in addition to waiting for the courts to grind on, the men behind the walls do form relationships with one another.

There are hates, loves, and accommodations. Jealousies, conspiracies and even ambitions lurk among this unique population. For some, prison is an emancipating experience, a place where they can almost 'come out of the closet'!

When the FBI began their interviewing program within the prison, they weren't sure the killers they most wanted to understand would even talk to them. And there's precious little an agent can do to either threaten or cajole a man who's already behind bars with enough consecutive life sentences to keep him there for eternity. Almost to their surprise, however, the sullen killers who'd clammed up to everyone, frequently including their own lawyers, prior to their incarceration were now quick to discuss even the most personal details of their lives! Still, it's not an easy process, as 'The Thin White Line' so aptly portrays.

When the FBI's agents began their interviews, they quickly discovered that at least half the interview occurred outside the interview room. Unless the agent was intimately familiar with the case, had a firm grasp of his subject, and

AS ALWAYS, FRANK
FINDS HIMSELF
RACING AGAINST
TIME

was prepared for the head games that most inmates enjoyed, the transcribed interview wasn't worth the paper it was printed on. Just as Hance attempted to substitute another inmate's history for his own, John Wayne Gacy frequently fed co-opted stories to the women who sent him groupie notes.

The fact that there were any stories to feed anyone was proof positive that inmates were regularly discussing their crimes among themselves. As sociologists like Abrams and Dean were to discover, 'There's a hierarchy among prisoners, based in part on the crimes they've been convicted of, in part on those they've managed to get away with, and in almost as great a part on the stature they can build in person. It's not unusual for details to get added to the truth as time goes on. A rapist, impressed by some comment overheard in jail about a completely disconnected crime, say a robbery, might later incorporate it into his own story, especially if he's transferred to a new facility where nobody knows the robbery guy's story.'

In an environment with such a skewed population, 'criminals suddenly find themselves in a situation where there's an acceptance of violence, where their fantasies aren't all that unusual, and where they can, for the very first time, talk openly with no chance of further reprisals. Just as mutual experiences and mutual confessions can bring a romantic couple closer together, the tight community inside a prison often produces intimate relationships.' Such was the case for Lawrence Bittaker and Roy Norris.

Bittaker and Norris might never have run into one another if it wasn't for the fact that both men, after convictions for a variety of crimes, ended up in the same prison. While chatting over old crimes through the bars, they discovered they shared a common fantasy: to catch, torture, sexually molest, and, in the ultimate show of control, kill women. Their shared dreams continued for the remainder of their incarceration – and beyond. Within weeks of their release, Bittaker and Norris met up in the City of Angels where they decided the time was right to put their dreams into action.

First, they purchased a roomy van which they dubbed 'Murder Mac', a vehicle with lots of room for their fun and games, and on 24 June, 1979, the fantasy turned real. Their victim was a beautiful sixteen-year-old named Cindy Schaeffer. After nabbing her just outside Redondo Beach, they bundled the terrified woman into their van and drove her into the mountains where they'd have even more privacy than in the confines of Murder Mac. Once there, they each raped her repeatedly, living out their sex-slave fantasy, delighting in her pain and fear, before they each took one end of an open wire coathanger and strangled her.

Andrea Joy Hall died with an ice-pick through her ear after being beaten and raped.

Jackie Gilliam and Leah Lamp, both only thirteen years old, were abducted together, tortured together over a 72-hour period, then, together, tossed over a cliff after being strangled.

Shirley Ledford, the next victim, had her brutalized body dumped on the front lawn of a Sunland home.

Ironically, it was Norris's boasting to yet another ex-con that would help police identify and convict both men, and, though both men had shared so much, Norris would prove Bittaker's ultimate undoing when he traded his testimony against his partner in exchange for a sentence that excluded the death penalty. Norris is still talking to his fellow inmates as he awaits his first chance for parole in 2010. Bittaker is talking to a different category of prisoner over on Death Row in San Quentin where he regularly makes up a foursome with 'Freeway Killer' William Bonin, the 'Sunset Strip Killer' Douglas Clark, and Randy Kraft who was convicted on sixteen counts of murder.

Wonder what they're talking about ...

Probably their records and the goings-on 'in the world' as they follow the careers of the media's latest fascination. Ted Bundy was certainly getting anxious during the Green River Killer's rampage. You'd think a man on Florida's Death Row would have any number of more immediate problems than the doings of a killer an entire continent away in Washington State, but Bundy, who was a notorious follower of his own press, is reputed to have commented that, 'the SOB is getting close, man, too damn close.' Bundy himself is known to have killed nineteen young women. The Green River Killer, who has never been identified, may have killed nearly fifty. But at the time that Bundy, apparently dissatisfied with both the FBI's progress and their profile, contacted the Bureau with an offer to help them track the killer, the confirmed count was closer to a dozen. Though agents did indeed talk with Bundy, the general feeling seems to have been that Bundy was more interested in the media interest in himself since making his Christmas-time offer. Fellow inmates snickered as they offered their own opinion of Bundy's fascination with the man, 'He's just afraid this guy'll outdo him and he knows he ain't getting an opportunity to up the score no more!'

The reverse relationship is also true. Just as killers on the inside follow the killings of those outside, those outside seem constantly aware of the various records held by those inside.

Both Donald Evans and Henry Lee Lucas have repeatedly changed, both up and down, the number of deaths each has claimed. Lucas's most extravagent claims, in the hundreds, prove impossible to confirm. His own recollections have put him in as many as three different locations at the same time. Donald Evans, who looked like a cop's gift, a guy willing to claim responsibility for dozens of unsolved homicides, has also turned out to be a braggart of the most pathetic sort with his personal goal being to outdo the media darling of the moment, Jeffrey Dahmer.

In looking for a cause for the apparent surge in serial killing, perhaps we need look no farther than ego.

NOTEBOOK:

GUEST FILMOGRAPHY:
JEREMY ROBERTS

Xena: Warrior Princess (1996) – Thercidese
Money Train (1995) – Guard
Hercules: The Legendary Journeys (1995) – Derk
Phoenix (1995) – Tanner
Star Trek: Voyager (1995) – Cmdr. Dimitri Valtane
Wing Commander IV (1995) – Lt Col Gash Dekker
The Mask (1994) – Bobby the Bouncer
The Adventures of Brisco County Jr (1993) – Bill Swill
Picket Fences (1993) – Carjacker
Diggstown (1992) – Sonny
The People Under the Stairs (1992) – Spenser
Sister Act (1992) – Biker #2
Seinfeld (1992) – The Chauffeur
Don't Touch My Daughter (1991) – Garnsey
False Arrest (1991) – Ed McCall
Late for Dinner (1991) – Truckdriver
The Marrying Man (1991) – Gus
Star Trek VI (1991) – Lt Dimitri Valtane
National Lampoon's Christmas Vacation (1989) – Cop
Peter Gunn (1989) – Slick

You Asked For It!

The bizarre psychology of the fictional Jacob Taylor, who believed his victims consented to their deaths, isn't fictional at all.

Waldemar Szczepinski, the 'Doorbell Killer' of West Berlin, rang the doorbells of old ladies all over the city. If they answered, his warped belief system told him it was fated that they be his victims. If they didn't answer, he just walked away. Like Jacob Taylor, the crimes lacked any sexual elements whatsoever. Jacob had a higher cause; Waldemar was just paying the mortgage. His reason for strangling a bunch of eighty-year-old women was the piddling amounts of money he could rummage from their apartments and purses.

Herbert Mullin was, without a doubt, mentally disturbed. Born into a religiously fanatical family, Herbert's every thought was extreme. The death of his best friend, Dean, became his lifelong tragedy. He turned his room into Dean's shrine. His very natural loneliness and grief became something twisted to him and he deduced that he must be a homosexual. After breaking off his engagement to his childhood sweetheart, he spent most of the next few years taking too many drugs and visiting mental hospitals in an effort to get rid of the 'voices in his head'.

Unfortunately, he wasn't in an institution when the voices started telling him to kill. Nor was there anyone nearby to tell him that the words his victims screamed as they died weren't 'I understand'.

HMMM, LET'S HOPE FRANK'S BREAKDOWN DIDN'T LEAD TO SCENES LIKE THIS!

TESTIMONY TRIVIA 14

QUESTIONS

Okay, the easy one-pointers first.

1 Whose picture is part of Frank Black's screensaver?
2 What did Frank find at the Rothenburg home that seems to have escaped the forensics team altogether?
3 What was Jacob Tyler's nickname in prison?
4 How many guards were required to bring Hance his meals?
5 How much did Jacob's purchases total at the Jet Grocery?

And now the tougher two-pointers.

6 When's Richard Hance's birthday?
7 What was the title of the fictional magazine seen by the delusional Jacob Tyler?
8 What fixture of his prison set-up did Hance particularly dislike?
9 Whose sob story did Hance 'borrow' and tell Black in an attempt to gain his sympathy?
10 How long did Hance figure it would take the guards to get inside the interview room?

Mullin, whose eyes and ears seemed as confused as Jacob's, remains convinced he should never have been convicted. In the first place, he was only carrying out God's instructions and, in the second, the sacrifices he made were willing.

INCIDENTALS:

Writers Morgan and Wong have long been known to weave in references to their favorite movies, television programs and, of course, their previous work. Allusions to their previous series, *Space: Above and Beyond*, were absolutely flying in this episode, much to the delight of the writers' fans.

The three cards found on victims, the Jack of Spades, King of Clubs and Queen of Hearts, correspond to the call-signs of the futuristic 58th Airborne in *S:AAB*. The 'Expect

LANCE HENRIKSEN
IN 'POWDER'

No Mercy' written on the back of each card was the squadron's motto.

Some viewers will also have found references to Morgan and Wong's career with *The X-Files*. How many members of the television audience watched Frank topple over a mattress standing in front of a hole in the wall and didn't yell, 'Watch out for Tooms!'? Or heard Frank tell Jacob Tyler, 'You are not who you are!' and didn't immediately remember another Morgan and Wong installment of *The X-Files* called 'Ice'?

□

Having Richard Hance relate his sob story of an illiterate youth to Lance Henriksen's character is something of an irony. Henriksen himself learned to read as an adult, a handy skill for a man who'd spend most of his life reading scripts.

ANSWERS

1   His daughter, Jordan's
2   Half a playing card
3   Mrs Hance
4   4
5   75 cents
6   17 February, 1953
7   *Captured*
8   The flourescent lights, they hummed
9   Willie Lloyd Turner, a convict executed on 25 May, 1995
10   33 seconds

YOUR SCORE:

CASE FILE: 'Sacrament'

CASE SYNOPSIS:

Tragedy strikes close when Helen Black is abducted outside the church where the Black clan has just celebrated the baptism of its newest member. Despite Bletcher's official and personal disapproval, and Catherine's serious concern, Frank pushes ahead with his private investigation – a search that will pit brother against brother.

LET'S HOPE THE SLOWLY EMERGING CIRCLE OF FAMILY ON *MILLENNIUM* DON'T MEET THE SAME POINTLESS FATE AS THE FAMILIES ON ANOTHER 10–13 PRODUCTION PROGRAM

KEY CITATION:

'Those tools you showed me were clean.
They weren't part of his torture kit, Bletch.
He was using them to hide the body.'

FRANK BLACK

VITAL STATISTICS:

Original US Airdate: 02/21/97

Production Number: 4C14
 Written by: Frank Spotnitz
 Directed by: Michael Watkins

Guest Cast:

Terry O'Quinn	Peter Watts
Stephen James Lang	Detective Giebelhouse
Brian Markinson	Detective Teeple
Liz Bryson	Helen Black
Philip Anglim	Tom Black
Dylan Haggerty	Richard Green
Daphne Goldrick	Green's Mother
Ken Roberts	Green's Father
Lorena Gale	Dr Patricia Moss
French Tickner	Store Clerk

Death Toll: None

CASE HISTORY:

THE DIY GUIDE TO GETTING RID OF BODIES

Traditionally, and in addition to their usual problems, serial killers faced two major obstacles. The first, finding and obtaining the perfect object of their perverse affections, could be, literally, just murder. The second, of course, was how to get rid of a partner who just wasn't living up to their end of the bargain – or living at all for that matter. In 'Sacrament', Mr Green the Elder solved the first problem by sending out Green the Junior to bring back whatever partners he could. Then, as any good father would, Green the Elder combined the necessity of ridding himself of Helen with a little shop class, both skills which would undoubtedly stand Green the Younger in good stead if Daddy had anything to do with the situation!

SHADES OF 'THE COUNT OF MONTE CRISTO'

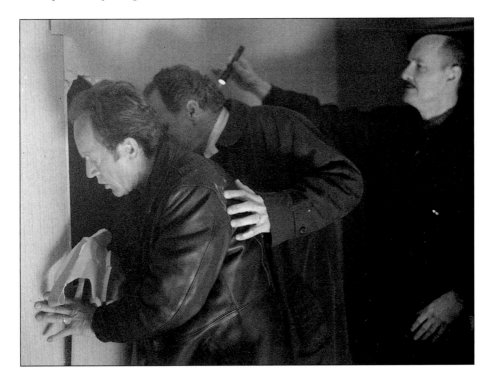

Still, while walling his victims up à la Count of Monte Cristo was certainly a classic choice, there is almost no limit to the options killers have managed to concoct over the years.

Serious Leery – yes, that's his real name – took inspiration from his work as a moving van driver and had his victims wrapped in plastic, palleted in sturdy wooden crates, and simply left them on his truck as 'part of one load or another' for nearly seven years. He'd likely have continued to get away with it (he'd murdered six people already, after all) if he hadn't had too large a nip at the pub with his lunch one day and delivered his latest victim instead of a set of Royal Doulton china to one of his job sites. He must still have been a bit punchy at supper. On being confronted by police that evening at home, his first concern was whether he was expected to pay for the 'missing' china out of his own pocket; his second concern centered on the likelihood of his having to take a breathalizer test which 'could cost me my job, ya know!'. The fate of Myra Lynch, the young woman he'd mistakenly delivered didn't bother him at all. 'There's no need to fuss, just tell me when'd be a convenient time for me to pick that box up in the morning.' He sobered up fairly quickly the next morning when the rest of his boxes were opened and he found himself facing six counts of first-degree murder.

Bathtubs have always been convenient places for messy jobs like washing the dog or re-potting that banana tree, so it's no surprise that serial killers have made equally good use of this convenient fixture and the equally convenient, not to mention flushable, fixture that's usually nearby.

To such use was bathroom piping put by Joachim Kroll who, like Leery, took inspiration from his job. In Joachim's case, the position of washroom attendant in a rooming house. When one of the tenants was questioned about a disappearance in the neighborhood, the young man had nothing to offer on the missing person, but did mention Joachim's warning to use the bathroom on the floor below as 'the one on this floor is bunged up with guts'. Needless to say, the police called a plumber. Within the hour, the toilet was yielding up its plug of body parts. Within minutes of that, police knocked down Joachim's door. Inside they found bag after bag of remains and, simmering in the oven, the hand of a four-year-old child. The ghoulish cannibal was convicted of 14 counts of murder, but could well have exceeded that.

In England, Dennis Nilsen was in-between lovers, and indulging in his favorite pastime, painting his body to look like a mutilated corpse and masturbating while staring at himself in a mirror. It wasn't long before he got himself a real corpse by the simple expedient of killing the young man he'd slept with the night before. Basically, Nilsen's claim was that he hated to be left alone, so, instead, he'd strangle his boyfriends, soap them up in a bubble bath, and keep them around as long as possible. When the decomposition became too advanced, well, like Kroll, he started tossing bits and pieces of his victims down the drain – and just about any-where else he could think of!

Nilsen started out like John Wayne Gacy, stuffing the remains under the floor, but, as he lived in a small flat, ran out of space rather quickly. A couple more were simply stuffed into a cupboard, a few more under a shed in the back garden – down the drain, however, quickly became his favorite disposal strategy. He'd already tried a bonfire in the backyard but, even after tossing on a few tires to smother the stench of burning flesh, the neighbors were too likely to call in the fire department to make that a viable strategy. Not sur-prisingly, Nilsen, like Kroll was done in by the discovery of human flesh in his drains.

CATCH IT? According to the files that just happened to cross Frank's desk, the most recent photo of Richard Green was taken on 11/23/88. Hasn't changed much has he?

Another classic is the lime pit, or, in modern times, the quicklime pit. It's esti-mated that since 1904, some 1250 people have been dissolved by lime. It's the seven who didn't dissolve, however, that point out the problem with quicklime as a disposal method. Though quicklime works wonderfully in damp spaces like the crawlway under Gacy's house, in the aqueous solution Dr H H Holmes favored in his own little basement hideaway, or in the open, outdoor vat of Saul Gantry who liked having somewhere to dump inconvenient women, it doesn't work at all without water!

Dorathea Puente should have read the instructions a bit more carefully before shaking the dry lime over the seven headless corpses she planted in her garden. Instead of dissolving the bodies, the quicklime kept them in fine condition until they could be dug up by some suspicious policemen who wondered where her borders were disappearing.

For instant satisfaction, there's nothing like fire. Up until recently, it was an almost fool-proof method to ensure no one discovered the precise identity of your victim, and, with nothing but a few bone and tooth fragments left afterwards, it certainly solved the space and storage problems. Still, it presented some unique problems of its own, like smell, which would undo Dr Marcel Petiot, and having a backyard crematorium was a sure way to rouse even the most lethargic police force's interest. Killer Deke Jacobson simply used the furnace in his apartment building's basement, being careful to feed just a limb or two a day to the roaring inferno, and never on Sunday morning because the building super cooled the machine Sunday evening to be emptied Monday morning. Deke killed three local vagrants and disposed of them without incident by following his own simple recipe; he was caught when he inadvertently killed a man in a post-barroom brawl on a Saturday night and couldn't come up with a place to hide him until Monday. The smell coming from his apartment alerted the tenants next door who called the police. As they arrived, Deke was caught literally red-handed, in the act of chopping up the body for consignment to the flames the following morning.

Funeral director murderers have a certain advantage over their fellow killers in the body disposal area, of course. Calvin Hobb of Chicago got so wrapped up in his hobby of raping, killing, mutilating and incinerating young streetwalkers that his boss, who owned the mortuary where he worked, once threatened to fire him for coming in late. The poor man never suspected the number of nights his young apprentice 'worked' over the crematory ovens, or why Calvin was so tired after 'an evening out'. Calvin, who hung with a rather odd crew anyway, had actually branched out, disposing of a variety of other people's corpses – for a fee. It started out simply enough with an arrangement between Hobb and a doctor who performed illegal abortions and wanted a better method of disposal. When one of the doctor's patients died from the procedure, it didn't take long for Hobb to come up

TESTIMONY TRIVIA 15

QUESTIONS

These are the easy ones!

1 What is Frank's nephew's name?
2 What did Frank once give his brother for Christmas?
3 What was missing from Tom and Helen's luggage?
4 What did Tom steal from his brother?
5 Who was the first to realize Helen Black was in trouble?

These will give you pause for thought.

6 In what church was the baptism held?
7 How did Richard Green attempt to disguise himself?
8 Where did Richard Green spend eight years of his life?
9 What did Frank find behind Green's bed?
10 What odd piece of evidence did Peter find in a car?

with a fee to cover the woman as well. When he was finally taken into custody, it's estimated he was handling a couple of corpses a week from local doctors and the remains of upwards of 40 abortions.

Obviously, the cleansing flames weren't an option for everyone and, in order to ensure that there was no chance of identifying the body if it was found, killers became an inventive lot. Marc DePaul ground up his mother-in-law's flesh, mixed it with corn mash and fed it to to his ducks. The bones he crushed and dug into his vegetable patch. It was the teeth he'd kept as something of a souvenir that did in this ambitious farmer!

Pigs regularly consumed the remains of Ed Goring's string of victims, right down to the bones, for nearly six years. When he moved on, leaving the pigfarm behind, he became a donator of 'meat and gristle' to the local Animal Protection League. Once, he even gained the gratitude of a men's shelter when he delivered 'four fine pots of stew' to them over the Christmas holidays.

Other animals proven efficient in the quick disposal of unwanted bodies have included geese and, unbelievable as it

sounds, alligators! Joe Ball, ex-bootlegger and owner of the
Sociable Inn, a dive of a drinking establishment in Texas,
installed a new attraction out back, a cement-pond full of
alligators. Clearly, with five of them in the one enclosure, no
one was about to try the 1930s emerging sport, 'gator-
wrestling, but they did serve a purpose other than upping the
macho-factor of the honky-tonk. Three Mrs Balls, a succession of gorgeous waitresses who all seemed inclined to provide Joe with whatever comfort they could, and even a yard
hand, all disappeared – or, as Joe kept assuring everyone
'they just moved on'. Sure, young women of the sort to take
jobs at the Sociable Inn in the first place, weren't the most
dependable of people, but, even the flightiest of young
women, like Hazel Brown, don't leave without their hard-
earned money! A deputy got suspicious and his suspicions
grew when Joe's neighbor started complaining about the foul
stench in the alligators' feed barrel.

Oh, so quietly, the deputy started asking around, trying to
find some sign of any of the eight missing people. He still
hadn't found any of them when yet another complaint about
the 'gators sent the police back to the Sociable Inn. Seeing as
he was there, the deputy decided to ask if Joe had heard from
Hazel lately. As another officer headed for the alligator
enclosure, Joe Ball reached up his counter, laid a pistol to his
head and blew his brains out.

The story was pieced together posthumously. Mrs Ball #3,
a very scared woman hiding out in San Francisco, confessed
that she knew of at least one woman who became food for
the 'gators but that she'd kept silent in order to escape the
same fate. It was Mrs Ball #3 who confirmed the location of
handyman Clifford Wheeler. From Wheeler, police learned
that Mrs Ball's fear was well-founded, it was Wheeler who'd
seen Joe dispose of one of the previous Mrs Balls! Very
shortly thereafter, he'd managed to gather together enough
free cash to take a good long trip away from Texas. He hadn't
dared sell anything to raise the money faster on the chance
Ball would figure out he was about to skip.

Poor Hazel Brown, the last waitress to disappear from the
Sociable Inn hadn't known about any of the first three Mrs
Balls when she started sleeping with her employer. By the

time she discovered she was pregnant, she'd also figured out that Joe wasn't about to do the 'honorable' thing and, before she could run, she joined two other pregnant women as food for the alligators.

Neils Barry, who also found himself in the embarrassing position of having both a wife and a pregnant mistress, didn't have a convenient cement-pond filled with hungry reptiles. Instead, he lured his young girlfriend out on a quiet evening for a walk among the hedgerows of the public gardens. They talked, he made extravagant promises, he nuzzled her neck, she nuzzled back, he found a quiet arbor off the main trail, they made love in the dappled moonlight under the trees,

GOTTA LOVE THAT SHIRT. WONDER IF IT'S LURKING AMID BLACK'S GRAY WARDROBE LIKE SOME GUILTY PLEASURE?

and then he shoved his lover into a wood-chipper before going home to his wife.

Glen Whitcomb had always been a creative child, a trait that served him well when, after a 'really bad date', he suddenly found himself with a corpse on his hands. His first attempt to dispose of the body was, well, less than successful. The rope he'd used to tie the body to an old V-8 engine before pushing it off the end of a wharf, slipped. She bobbed to the surface before he could even get back to his car. An attempt to burn the body in his building's furnace wasn't particularly successful either. The entire body wouldn't fit, but, instead of cutting her into two more manageable pieces, he tried to burn off her feet and slowly shove her in a bit further. He quickly discovered just what a stench a burning body makes and, terrified that someone would come to investigate, he dragged the partially burned, partially water-logged, body from the makeshift oven, put her back into the trunk and went cruising, looking for a more likely way to rid himself of the erstwhile love of his life.

Maybe he'd been watching too many gangster movies, or maybe the construction site he happened across just looked too good, but Whitcomb wasted no time in mixing up a bit of concrete and adding his girlfriend to the foundation of the about-to-be erected community center. Unfortunately for him, however, the foreman on the site was an observant guy and he was pretty sure he hadn't overseen any work in that area the previous day. Maybe he watched too many gangster movies too. In any case, he called in the police who prodded through the new layer of concrete and turned up the half-burned body. It took them about 52 minutes to track her back to Whitcomb. So secure had he felt in this last resting place that he'd tossed her purse in with her. Her roommate gave police his name and address almost immediately.

Next to these impressarios, tossing bodies into rivers, shallow graves and roadside ditches seems just ... mundane.

ANSWERS

Take a single point for each correct answer.

1. Charles Francis Black
2. A bicycle
3. A baggage tag
4. Frank's gun
5. Jordan Black

Two points for each of these.

6. St John's Church
7. He wore a wig
8. Glenrosa State Hospital for the Criminally Insane
9. A satanic symbol scratched into the wall
10. A piece of a Japanese cedar

YOUR SCORE:

NOTEBOOK:

GUEST FILMOGRAPHY:
KEN ROBERTS (MR GREEN)

Deadlocked: Escape from Zone 14 (1995) – Penal Officer
Deceptions II: Edge of Deception (1995)
– Captain Harrelson
Bullets Over Broadway (1994) – Theatre Well-Wisher
Don't Talk to Strangers (1994) – Murdoch
Exquisite Tenderness (1994) – County General Guard
Flinch (1994) – Security Guard
Flight From Justice (1993) – Dimitri
A Cry in the Night (1992) – Mr Hartley
Double Identity (1990) – Mr Crawley
Murder One (1988) – Store Keeper
The Great Land of Small (1987) – Flannigan/Munch
Radio Days (1987) – The Radio Voice
Wild Thing (1987) – Bugs
Junior (1985) – Sheriff
Lune De Miel (1985) – Snack Bar Customer

CASE FILE: 'Walkabout'

CASE SYNOPSIS:

Catherine and Peter worry that Frank is slipping towards yet another breakdown when, after assuming the name of a dead childhood friend, he disappears for two days. His reappearance in a back alley, with no memory of his whereabouts – but a deep-seated certainty that he's been involved in a murder, does nothing to ease any of their minds!

FRANK'S PAST REMAINS A QUESTION, BUT WHAT ANSWERS CAN VIEWERS EXPECT IF CATHERINE FEARS EPISODES LIKE THIS ARE A 'RECURRENCE'?

KEY CITATION:

'I don't know what all the stink is all about. Believe me, I saw much worse down in New Orleans. Some kind of anti-Alzheimer concoction that they're trying to sneak past the FDA. Everyone was crazycorn for a whole week afterwards!'

MOXIE

VITAL STATISTICS:

Original US Airdate: 03/28/97

Production Number: 4C15
   Written by: Chip Johannessen
                    Tim Tankosic
   Directed by: Cliff Bole

Guest Cast:

Terry O'Quinn	Peter Watts
Stephen James Lang	Detective Giebelhouse
Nancy Kerr	Personnel Chief Flender
Zeljko Ivanek	Dr Daniel Miller
Greg Itzin	Hans Ingram
Ron Suave	Tardot
Alison Matthews	Sandy Geiger
Dee Jay Jackson	G.J.
Arthur Corber	Moxie
Cheryl Mullen	Sal
Kym Sheppard	Trial Nurse

Death Toll: 1 female, beaten to death
                                        1 male, drug-induced vehicular victim
                                        1 male, drug-induced suicide
                                        4 gender unknown, drug-induced murder/suicide

CASE HISTORY:

IT AIN'T WORTH $1.73 NO MORE !

Once upon a time, in an effort to teach us what a paltry place we occupied in the Grand Scheme of Things, biology teachers fondly explained that, after taking out the 70% of us that was water, grinding and separating what was left, and selling the useful minerals for their present market value, the entire human body would be lucky to net $1.73. Talk about short-sighted! Though little

THE LAST CASE FRANK, PETER AND BOB WOULD WORK TOGETHER

known and little discussed, there is an entire employment group making lots more than that from their bodies! Who are they? Why, the same 'human guinea pigs' that so startled Peter Watts in Dr Danny's apartment, of course.

And they're going about it in the most inventive ways!

Gone are the days when profit-oriented individuals with healthy bodies to market were limited to queueing in line with the winos to sell a pint of blood. Now, organized plasma centers have sprung up across the United States with scheduled donations by registered donators who can earn up to $200 per month for simply rolling up their sleeves every three to five days! And that's not all they can sell – not by a long shot. Sperm banks, chronically short of a good variety of donors, offer $40–$60 per donation. Not bad for a relatively painless procedure that's repeatable as often as ten times per month while still adhering to the 'three days between' mandate that will keep the necessary counts high.

The complementary procedure for women, while considerably more painful, pays even better, up to $2500 per month. The market for body parts, like any other market, varies in its desires and its pricing, but, at this time, the raw material for high-tech reproductive strategies are certainly lucrative. Hair, which used to bring big bucks back at the turn of the century, is only being purchased by a few companies and the price, considering the time it takes most people to grow twelve inches of it, hardly makes it a worthwhile endeavor.

No, for serious, regular income, human guinea pigs have two main opportunities available. The first is the outright sale of body organs. As that practice occasions a certain degree of moral outrage in some quarters, the second, participation in drug and therapy trials, is the most common and consistent way for the professional human guinea pig to make a living.

Just as test pilots tend to make more than commercial pilots who follow the same milk-run six days a week, the riskier or just generally more unpleasant the trial, the more money the guinea pig is likely to make. In the world of legitimate clinical drug trials, trials progress in an organized fashion that must follow the guidelines established by the FDA.

That's to avoid situations that kill 100 people in 15 states, as happened when Elixir Sulfanilamide went on the market. It contained diethylene glycol, a sweet-tasting compound that's also found in, get this!, anti-freeze. In 1938, the FDA began organizing a clinical trial system that's been refined in an ongoing process ever since. Along the way, and after some spectacular foul-ups, a number of laws were passed to protect the test subjects as well as anyone slugging down the drug company's latest concoction.

BLOOPER! Just can't figure out that puddle of blood. It was dripping away, making a little pinkish splotch, but, in the time it took Peter Watts to blink twice, it grew to a puddle bigger than a big man's hand and turned almost black!

The first human trial phase (Phase 1 Testing), is the riskiest. The only pre-requisite for human testing is that the drug already pass through enough animal testing to prove it isn't lethal to two other species. There's really nothing to say that what's safe for mice or chickens is safe for human beings, of course … And, the only real question being answered in Phase 1 Testing is: does it kill people? If, in the process of answering the primary question, the first trial also brings out potential problems, like some of the truly nasty side-effects, among them rashes or brain seizures, well, that's always nice to know, but it just isn't the first order of business. That can be a disconcerting thought for a lot of people.

As can all the 'inconveniences' that go with being a test subject. First, guinea pigs must prove they're healthy when they begin the trial. The proof usually entails being jabbed in various locations, having rubber gloves inserted in other locations, and being generally poked and prodded almost everywhere else. Depending on the trial, the routine checks to assess the drugs' effects, which could include blood and urine sampling or any of the previously mentioned poking and prodding, might be once a week, once a day, or even, horror of horrors, hourly.

It's not the sort of job that you can just drop out of whenever you choose either. Though being a test subject generally pays pretty well, the payment scheme is often arranged such that, if you drop out early, you get absolutely nothing. At the very least, you'll lose a significant portion of what pay you might have expected. If there's no ill effect, it's pretty easy money; if you're one of the ones with the hives, or worse, it can be pure hell.

So why do people do it? Why put up with the almost military school conditions imposed by most studies? Or the physical discomfort? Or the mind-altering side-effects? For most people, it's strictly for the money. Depending on the riskiness of the drug, and the position of the company ordering the trial, subjects can receive up to $250 a week, plus, of course, all their food, and a place to sleep. Test subjects, as a sort of bonus, are also getting some of the best medical care possible! By the time the trial is over, many subjects are not only a bit richer, but healthier!

Some subjects would participate for nothing, however, as was the case for James Muro who loaned out his body, gratis, for Phase 1 Testing that both he and the drug company hoped would lead to an AIDS cure. Muro, whose sister died of the disease two years ago, has been a Phase 1 subject for nine different AIDS treatments. 'Some of them were pretty horrid, but, I guess I'm hoping that one of them will ensure that no one else I know, no one else I love, has to die that way. Nothing, no side-effects, could be worse than that.'

For others, like Terrence Whittiker, the cause is even more personal. Diagnosed with AIDS just last year, Whittiker has volunteered for every related drug testing trial he could find. Though he doesn't fit the John Q Public profile needed for Phase 1 Testing, later testing requires the company to prove the drugs are not only non-lethal, but that they have some effect on the disease or condition the drug is supposed to address. It's this later, Phase 2 and 3 Testing that drew Whittiker. 'I've got next to nothing to lose and if, by some miracle, they actually find something that works, that makes me even a little better, they are required by law to continue letting me have that drug – even if it's not on the market yet!' He's right, and, considering how long it can take a drug to get to market, time Whittiker realistically admits he hasn't got, this is about the only way he'll ever get to try cutting-edge treatments.

Still, while other motives for participation aren't hard to find, most subjects are paid guinea pigs and happy to continue in their unusual profession. Mark Guillicutty has been a subject for six years. 'It's great if you're single, if you like to move

---

TESTIMONY TRIVIA 16

QUESTIONS

These are the easy ones!

1 What alias did Frank use in his e-mail correspondence?
2 Who was two weeks late on the rent for Apt 109?
3 What drug was being tested?
4 What was unusual about David Marx's hospital records?
5 What was found in the doctor's 'fridge?

And these will make you think!

6 Name the clinic where the drug tests were conducted.
7 How did Dr Danny diagnose Frank's condition?
8 How old is Frank?
9 What date did 'David Marx' give as his birthday?
10 What company funded the trials?

---

around the country, if you like to decide when you're going to holiday. I'm pretty free right now. I've got plenty of money to live on and it lets me do some things that other people never get to fit into their nine-to-five schedules.' Among those 'things' that Mark's managed to work in are twelve off-Broadway plays that received good enough reviews to land him an agent. He's currently plugging away at a full-production version of one of those plays for spring production in Stratbourne, organizing his notes for his next teaching seminar in September, and continuing to 'read all those books I'd never be able to cram into my lunch hour if I was still, you know, "working".' Prior to becoming a writer-cum-guinea pig, Mark was a trader at the New York Stock Exchange. 'I'd rather scratch for a few days and know I can take my vacation when everyone else is stuck in the city than go back to the Ex.'

Mark may be happy with his lifestyle and the payments he receives, but other professional guinea pigs want a little more for the use of their unique services and, for about 1200 people a year, that means enrolling themselves in the renegade trials that are neither approved by the FDA nor reviewed by the Institute Review Boards, the in-house voices of reason for large companies and testing facilities.

Are they dangerous? Yes, of course, especially if you've no practical knowledge of what you're getting into. Are they more dangerous than regular studies? Sometimes yes, sometimes no. There are two basic reasons why a study might be a renegade. The first and most obvious is that no one with a brain cell to call their own would fund it through normal channels! While looking for work in one university's Psychology Department – incidently, a great place to pick up odd jobs like seeing how fast you can sort cards after five beers – Frank Trainer saw a rather interesting note on the bulletin board.

Naturally, he checked with the contact number given, wondering why they didn't have subjects coming out the whazoo. The 'study' involved being chilled to the point of unconsciousness, left overnight, then being thawed out the next day. Equally naturally, Trainer decided to pass.

WANTED

Subjects for the Coolest Study on Campus!

$100 a Day!

Just three days!

Then there are the studies that simply don't apply to enough people to bring in the big research bucks that would support a full-scale Four Phase study. Take the rare condition known as Weiss-Rohmman's Syndrome, which affects the clichéd one-in-a-million people. While it's not high on the list of diseases that pharmaceutical companies are anxious to investigate, it's vitally important to the handful of people in the United States that share the syndrome. Paul Hodder took part in one of the renegade studies dedicated to alleviating the symptoms of Weiss-Rohmman's without incurring any extra danger whatsoever. He was better paid and, in his experienced opinion, better treated during this study than he'd been in any other. 'When you're into an FDA-style study, you know the trial organizers are required by law to tell you absolutely everything they know so they can get your signature on that Informed Consent document. The people at the renegade study were every bit as diligent, they even brought in outside experts to answer my questions. I went to my own doctor with their study outline and all the information and,

frankly, even he couldn't see anything in the least suspicious.' At the end of the trial, Paul was $3000 in pocket for a week's work and felt he'd done something really worthwhile.

Not all renegade studies turn out so well, however. Jules Rioux will never again participate in anything without all the official seals of approval. 'I signed up for what I thought was a simple study. It was for a new painkiller, which I recognized was likely to be an hallucinogenic, most of the heavier drugs like morphine and demerol have that possibility. But, I'll be honest, I had no idea what I was getting into this time. I knew I was in trouble when I started seeing the arms reaching up out of the floor to get me ... I screamed for one of the attendants, I know that much. But, I think I must have screamed for hours after that and there was nothing, no one, to help me. By the time I came down, I think it was two days later, I was in real trouble. I'd torn open these huge gashes in my arms and legs, almost torn off one earlobe. I'm pretty sure I hadn't had anything to drink in that time either, so I wasn't very steady. They took me to a hospital and dropped me off, that was it. I was ready to take them to court, but, I'd signed off on the consent and, well, what happened to me was within the possible parameters of the study. It stinks, but, there it is.'

It's studies gone wrong, trials like Jules's, that open the door to the same abuse of subjects that the laws were meant to stop. And, if you're a writer for *Millennium*, it's the sort of almost-true-story that makes for a delightfully horrifying episode.

NOTEBOOK:

On A Need To Know Basis

Though amnesia isn't as commonplace as soap operas would have us believe, it does pop up from time to time, usually as a result of head injury or trauma. Only rarely does a drug, commercially or clinically available, cause memory loss as happened in 'Walkabout'.

When an amnesiac first turns up, it's usually at a police station or in a hospital, somewhere where they believe they'll find help, so, when a 36-year-old man turned up at a police station in Hamburg, Germany, the officers were startled but hardly stymied and quickly began trying to reunite Mr X with his past. Their grateful client was less gracious two days later when they announced that they knew exactly who he was – and snapped the cuffs on him. They'd discovered he was wanted for fraud and larceny!

In Trevise, Italy, a young girl who appeared to have been involved in some sort of car accident was brought from the scene to an emergency room where it became evident that she had no idea who she was. Using the license plate to trace her parents, they told her she was Adele Avoniconi and started looking for her closest relations. That happened to be a couple in upstate New York who, having left Italy some nine years ago, had never seen the child. In any case, young Adele lived with the couple for the next sixteen years then, after herself being involved in a car accident, suddenly looked up at her doctor and announced, 'My name is Greta Krohl.' Much to everyone's surprise, she was right. The Krohls had reported her missing, kidnapped, at about the right time and pictures quickly confirmed her identity. The destroyed car had been her kidnapper's, not her parents and she'd been living with her abductor's sister without ever realizing it.

The record for the longest period of amnesia that resulted in a recovery likely belongs to Marie-Claude Valcour of Paris. In 1915, she was visiting an aunt when a bomb exploded in the nearby barn. Her aunt was killed and, in the turmoil surrounding the incident, the child, whom neighbors didn't recognize and who didn't recall anything about herself, was put into foster care. Shortly thereafter, the entire village was evacuated and Marie-Claude's parents were unable to locate her. Seventy-two years later, an elderly woman walked up to a boarded up house and quietly assured the grandson holding her elbow that 'Yes, this is where I lived.' She'd finally remembered her address.

ANSWERS

Take a single point for each correct answer.

1 David Marx
2 Dr Daniel Miller
3 Proloft. Sound familiar? Think Prozac and Zoloft!
4 It was full of blank paper
5 A lot of green apples and a dead patient

These tougher questions will earn you two points each.

6 The Whole Family Health Clinic
7 Selective retrograde amnesia, possibly psychogenic
8 49
9 21 July, 1947
10 Bedford Shriver Pharmaceuticals

YOUR SCORE:

GUEST FILMOGRAPHY:
ZELJKO IVANEK (DR DANNY)

Donnie Brasco (1997) – Tim Curley
The Associate (1996) – SEC Agent Thompkins
Courage Under Fire (1996) – Banacek
Infinity (1996) – Bill Price
White Squall (1996) – Sanders
The X-Files: Roland (1994) – Roland
Homicide: Life on the Street (1993) – ASA Ed Danvers
School Ties (1992) – Cleary
Aftermath: A Test of Love (1991) – Matt
Our Sons (1991) – Donald
Echoes in the Darkness (1987) – Vince Valaitus
Rachel River (1987) – Momo
Mass Appeal (1984) – Mark Dolson

INCIDENTALS:

'I don't even take aspirin.'

Indicative of a rather pronounced change of focus for this episode, that line came from Henriksen who strongly objected to the original script's implication that Frank Black would deliberately take any type of drug much less one that had yet to be proven in legitimate trials.

HOW MANY MARRIAGES COULD STAND SCENES LIKE THIS MORE THAN ONCE?

CASE FILE: 'Covenant'

CASE SYNOPSIS:

When Frank is called in to assess the mind of a man who's already confessed to, and been convicted of, murdering his wife and his three children, the prosecutor wants a profile that'll ensure William Garry receives the death penalty. He's none too pleased when Frank's investigations start suggesting they've jailed the wrong man.

FRANK FINDS HIMSELF IN AN UNUSUAL POSITION IN 'COVENANT'
– TRYING TO CONVINCE THE CONVICT TO ADMIT HIS INNOCENCE

KEY CITATION:

'Frank, the last thing those children saw, before they saw the face of God, was their father's face – the face of a murderer. I want William Garry to pay for that.'

CALVIN SMITH

VITAL STATISTICS:

Original US Airdate: 03/21/97

Production Number: 4C16
    Written by: Robert Moresco
    Directed by: Rod Pridy

Guest Cast:

Don Mackay	Jack Meredith
Steve Bacic	Deputy Kevin Reilly
John Finn	William Garry
Colleen Winton	Mrs Garry
Tyler Thompson	William Garry Jr
Nikol Tschenscher	Mary Garry
Cody Shaer	Gabriel Garry
Nicole Oliver	Dr Alice Steele
Sarah Koskoff	Dr Didi Higgins
Michael O'Neil	Calvin Smith
David Abbott	Mr Anderson
Karen Elizabeth Austin	Mrs Anderson
Noah Heney	Charles Horvath
Jay Underwood	Slattery
George Gordon	Judge Francis Maher
Norman Armour	Medical Examiner

Death Toll: 1 female adult, suicide
                 1 female child, stabbed
                 2 male children, stabbed

CASE HISTORY:

FANTASY, REALITY AND PERCEPTION

It's no surprise that an entire series devoted to a character whose perceptions are 'different' than ours, who chases criminals who see things 'differently', criminals that may well be something other than they appear, should, from time to time, create episodes seemingly designed to challenge our perspective. 'Covenant' is never entirely what it appears to be. It constantly asks us to wrap our heads around a new interpretation of events, to see a done deal from yet another viewpoint, denouncing our concepts of facts and truth – all while continuously grounding this episode in a myriad of little 'truths' that fix it firmly in time and place.

It was no accident that this episode was set in Utah. While images of firing squads and of blood seeping into the ground seem barbaric in a time when Prisoner Rights and the benchmark of 'cruel and unusual' means a 400-pound man can't be executed by hanging on the chance he'd be decapitated, Utah's adherence to its 'right' to offer the condemned man, or woman, the firing squad startles audiences almost from the opening sequence. A little throw-back, something of an anachronism to remove the action from the too-well known settings of California and New York, undermining the audience's assurance that they knew what was coming, they knew what laws were at work.

Compounding the audience's sense of alienation is William Garry himself. His determination to die, so completely at odds with the recent, highly-publicized struggles by a number of real criminals, not to mention big-screen film portrayals, immediately sets him apart, giving his character a roundness seldom seen in traditional cop shows. His failure to fit the criminal-protesting-his-innocence stereotype allowed for new, different scenes to be played out. No sleazy lawyers here – on either side. The prosecutor, believing sincerely in Garry's guilt, makes no bones about wanting a monster not only out of the system, but out of the world! The defence is equally convincing as the outraged moralist on the last frontier; only in Utah do defense attorneys have clients being literally shot. In a society that likes to sanitize its executions, this setting grounds viewers in the reality of violent death, not just for victims but for perpetrators, while simultaneously emphasizing how different capital punishment is where the majority of viewers live – not in Utah!

Garry's religious beliefs are equally capable of removing him from our general comprehension. Who believes in religious covenants anymore? Especially ones with such drastic and inconvenient traditions! The last time America was confronted with so sincere a religious fanatic, they were being horrified by the grandfatherly figure of Albert Fish. This hunched little old man was the epitome of a book that couldn't be read by its cover. Most famous for the 1928 kidnapping and murder of twelve-year-old Grace Budd, Fish not only killed the girl, he took select portions of her body home to make stew which he ate while masturbating compulsively. And she was only one of his victims! Though Fish's crimes added up to an abominable criminal career, certainly enough to give normal people nightmares, it was Fish's own justifications, his own warped logic, that truly made him a 'monster', a creature beyond our understanding, because Fish was, to the end, a religious man!

It was his 'atonement' for his sins that so few could, or will, understand. Like Garry, he truly did feel guilt, but, where Garry's was an innocent man's assumption of a guilt for which he was only remotely responsible, Fish, guilty in every sense, believed he could 'become innocent' again by acknowledging God's punishments and indulging in masochistic rites that didn't even have names at the time. His claim to have atoned for Grace Budd's death by inserting five needles through his scrotum into his abdomen was so bizarre that police originally dismissed it as a delusional fantasy or a

BLOOPER! How did Mrs Garry manage to get through an autopsy without the coroner realizing she was pregnant? Considering the portrayal of the Prosecutor, it's not possible that he'd decide not to use that knowledge in the trial or penalty phase.

TESTIMONY TRIVIA 17

QUESTIONS:

1 What decorating motif was found throughout the house?
2 How does Frank like his coffee?
3 What did Garry buy for his youngest child on the day he was born?
4 What was written on the base of the angel Garry made for his wife's birthday?
5 What was written on the rock thrown through Frank's windscreen?
6 What was written on the plaque over Garry's workbench?
7 What number was written on the window?
8 Name any two of the Garry children.
9 What did Mrs Garry buy at the pharmacy the night she died?
10 What's Mrs Garry's first name?

pathetic attempt to gain sympathy. The truth, that Fish had 29 needles floating about in his lower abdomen – some actually beginning to rust! – placed him firmly in the realm of aliens. The remaining litany of self-flagellation, pubic burnings and the even more bizarre, forcing of rose stems up his penis to be either ripped out in one excruciating spasm or slowly to extend his self-torture, seemed somehow less horrendous because, by then, absolutely no one could identify with Albert Fish. Garry's efforts at penitence never took him to Fish's extremes, but his desire for death, a bloody death he hadn't earned, kept him removed from viewers, providing them an anti-hero where they'd expected something altogether different.

Bringing the very real Arthur Shawcross into the arguments played out in this fictitious milieu set viewers up for yet another warp of reality. Shawcross is famous less for his impressive body count than for the fact it was racked up over two separate killing streaks with his worst atrocities happening after being jailed once and then paroled. Comparing Garry to Shawcross, who killed for reasons as compelling as having his prostitute partner laughing during sex, sets up a definite image for the audience, an image that also turns out to have no basis in reality.

The 'reality' of the truth is called into question more blatently when Frank Black calls in a polygrapher. The polygraph, the absolute bane of judges everywhere since Daubert opened the door to the inclusion of dozens of soft sciences, is stirring up just as much trouble now as it did when first introduced by the same man who created Wonder Woman and gave her a golden lasso that compelled those caught in its coils to tell the truth. It has notorious admissibility problems, and a distinct lack of reliable scientific trials to confirm its veracity. Everyone acknowledges polygraph machines register metabolic response, but, though Americans perceive almost any gizmo with buttons, flashing lights, and little pens tracing out what appears to be a mathematically significant and quantifiable result, there's no study to prove it's measuring truth.

IS THAT A SMILE?

That Frank would resort to such inconclusive methods to convince himself of Garry's mindset is, in itself, a way of changing our perception of him. Why would Frank Black need such confirmation when the evidence itself, even without the benefit of his special form of perception, is already illustrating holes in the prosecution story? Just who was going to be convinced by unreliable methods? Perhaps it's because the evidence itself forced Frank to re-examine that evidence, because it was the hard facts that he couldn't quite resolve?

Some things are, without doubt, outside our common understanding of humanity as a species. Few of us could conceive of a woman – especially a woman – murdering her three living children, her unborn child, and herself! The case of Smith, who drowned both her children in a car she claimed

had been high-jacked, left America staggered by the mere idea that a woman could commit so callous a crime against her own children, with no apparent signs of remorse! In an episode that kept pushing us past our prejudices, we were also forced to reverse the roles we've come to accept as almost normal. There was no violent, philandering husband. There was no moment of rage that led to murder, no history of violence, no abused wife cut down while protecting her children. None of our casual assumptions held up, not even the coroner's evidence was clear. The final revelation, that Garry was as much a victim as his children stuns viewers who'd already discovered they'd followed a dozen red herrings.

Given an on-going theme of careless perceptions and broken stereotypes, Mrs Garry's personal vision, delusional as it was, takes on a certain sanity and viewers find themselves almost empathizing with the true murderer! If episodes 10–13 set out to demolish our stereotypes and make us question our reason, 'Covenant' certainly succeeded by playing fast and loose with the edge of reality.

NOTEBOOK:

GUEST FILMOGRAPHY:
JOHN FINN (WILLIAM GARRY)

Turbulence (1997) – Sinclair
NYPD Blue (1997) – Lt Shannon
The X-Files (1997) – Michael Kritschcau
EZ Streets (1996) – Captain Geary
City Hall (1996) – Commissioner Coonan
Blown Away (1994) – Captain Roarke
Carlito's Way (1993) – Duncan
Cliffhanger (1993) – Agent Michaels
Geronimo: An American Legend (1993) – Captain Hentig
Nowhere to Run (1993) – Cop in Chase
The Pelican Brief (1993) – Matthew Barr
Citizen Cohn (1992) – Senator Charles Potter
Steel Justice (1992) – Bill Somes
Flying Blind (1992) – Mr Rickman
I Posed for Playboy (1991) – Jimmy Lanahan
Cover-Up (1990) – Jeff Cooper
Desperate Hours (1990) – Lexington
Loose Cannons (1990) – Cop
A Shock to the System (1990) – Motorman
Glory (1989) – Sergeant Mulcahy
Alone in the Neon Jungle (1988) – Benson
Shakedown (1988) – Bartender
The Pope of Greenwich Village (1984) – Ginty
Funny Bones (1995) – Blackpool Unit Manager

INCIDENTALS:

Though the United States has more prisoners on Death Row than any other country, a number of states have no death penalties: Alaska, District of Columbia, Hawaii, Iowa, Maine, Massachusetts, Michigan, Minnesota, North Dakota, Rhode Island, Vermont, West Virginia, and Wisconsin.

☐

Check out the closed captioning for this episode and you'll notice that the questions put to William Garry have nothing to do with the questions filmed in the polygraph scene. Instead of 'Is your name William Garry?' the question reads 'Are you currently in Vancouver?' Instead of 'Were you a Weeber County sheriff?' it asks 'Are you an actor?' That's one way to get a 'Yes' response.

ANSWERS

1   An angel theme
2   Black
3   A plush elephant
4   'Love Bill'
5   Guilty
6   'If a man fails at home, he fails in life'
7   12815
8   William Jr, Mary, and Gabrielle. Take three points if you got them all right
9   A bottle of cough syrup and a home pregnancy test
10 Dolores

YOUR SCORE:

HOW LONG WILL IT BE BEFORE CATHERINE'S SMILE GRACES THE YELLOW HOUSE AGAIN?

CASE FILE: 'Lamentation'

CASE SYNOPSIS:

Frank Black's former FBI colleagues in Washington waste no time calling him in again when a prisoner he once caught – and later saved from the executioner – escapes. As if trying to work while second guessing his previous decisions isn't difficult enough, Frank can't help noticing that Dr Fabricant's latest games include disturbing references to Frank's home and family.

KEY CITATION:

'I know this man and I know what drives him.
Dr Fabricant told me, as a boy, he used to slit the stomachs of neighborhood cats and turn 'em loose
– just to see how long they'd live. After med school, as a resident, he would respond to no-code patients just to see how they died. He said the medical profession had but one interest for him, the knowledge and the opportunity to rend death from life. His appetite for death eventually became overwhelming, ending in the murder-torture of the five nurses in Cedar Falls. It has been six years since he has touched, tasted, or indulged his interests. He would not let so easy an opportunity get away.'

FRANK BLACK

VITAL STATISTICS:

Original US Airdate:	04/18/97
Production Number:	4C117
Written by:	Chris Carter
Directed by:	Winrich Kolbe

Guest Cast:

Terry O'Quinn	Peter Watts
Stephen James Lang	Detective Giebelhouse
Michael David Simms	Special Agent Tom Babich
Jane Perry	Agent Pierce
Nino Caratozzolo	Agent Cuevas
Kurt Max Runte	The Federal Marshall
Andrew Arlie	Dr Willmore
David Mackay	The Pathologist
Alex Diakun	Dr Ephraim Fabricant
Lee Van Paassen	Sondra Fabricant
Sarah Jane Redman	Lucy Butler

Death Toll:	1 male, throat cut

CASE HISTORY:

THE DOCTORS OF DEATH

Considering the number of spectacular murderers who've come from the ranks of the 'caring professions', the doctors, nurses, pharmacists, and even social workers who've made their clients their preferred prey, the level of trust we as a society still place in these authoritarian figures is almost absurd. Of course, the vast majority of

health care and community professionals are just that, caring individuals whose primary concern is for their patients, but, the small serial killing minority cut such colorful characters, commit such horrendous acts, they've become something of a special area of study in an already flamboyant group.

The very first American serial killer, at least as defined by the FBI parameters, the horrific 'H H Holmes', was as notorious in his day as Jeffrey Dahmer is in ours. A contemporary of Jack the Ripper, who many believe must have had some medical experience of his own, the dapper Dr H H Holmes was actually born Herman Mudgett, a moniker few could blame him for dropping at the first opportunity. It was as 'little Herman' that Holmes tortured and killed all the neighborhood critters he could get his hands on, calling his bizarre pastime 'medical experiments'. He hung one cat from a tree branch, slit open just the skin of its stomach and left it there, checking back from time to time to see if it was still alive.

While the 'Holmes' part of his new identity was completely fraudulent, a move to separate himself from his past, a past that included a wife he now found inconvenient, the 'Doctor' title was his by honest labor. He graduated high in his class from the University of Michigan at Ann Arbor in 1884. It was during his time at medical school, when he had legitimate access to a variety of corpses, that he hit on the first of his gory money-making schemes. After taking out an insurance policy on some fictitious person, he'd wait until a corpse fitting the general age-condition particulars on the policy came along, then rename the corpse and collect on the insurance. To the best of any authority's knowledge, he hadn't yet made the jump to finding a living person of the right type and creating a suitable corpse. He appears to have been motivated by greed, a need that was being satisfied.

When he moved to Chicago a few years later, he left Mudgett behind, adopted the name Henry Howard Holmes, and continued his scheming ways. First, he took a position as a medical chemist, a druggist, at a small business in a very comfortable neighborhood. He could have taken up several equally nice jobs, but this one had a distinct advantage – the owner was a widow who'd fallen for Holmes's brand of charm. Not surprisingly to anyone who knew him, the widow soon disappeared and left Holmes the pharmacy. For many men, that would have been enough, but H H Holmes had bigger plans.

Using his refined con skills on a wide group of 'investors', Holmes soon amassed enough free cash to begin building a palatial residence across from his new business. While many people admired the outside of the structure, few people realized just how unusual it would be inside. By switching workers frequently and supervising the construction personally, Holmes managed to install some unique amenities without arousing any suspicion whatsoever, among them peepholes, a series of secret passages connecting rooms, trap doors that dropped unsuspecting 'guests' into the cellar, soundproofing sufficient to eliminate even the screams of his most recalcitrant visitors, pipes that led to numerous rooms throughout the house, rooms that were also conveniently airtight, and a fully-equipped lab downstairs which included a number of efficiently laid out dissection tables.

Though many people came to visit 'The Castle', there were an alarmingly few who could actually say they'd been inside and come out again.

Even while Holmes indulged all the sick fantasies he could come up with, he remained true to his money-grubbing roots and it's not at all coincidental that, while Holmes remained a free man in Chicago, local medical schools had an unending supply of beautifully mounted skeletons as well as medical cadavers. The World Fair of 1893, held in Chicago, when Holmes opened his huge house as a temporary 'boarding house', resulted in an almost embarrassing wealth of high-grade lab specimens – and who was to say what happened to some hicks spending their first vacation in the big city?

Unbelievable as it seems in retrospect, nearly thirty people disappeared inside the Castle and absolutely no one suspected anything! If Holmes hadn't returned to his original scheme, the insurance fraud, and done something to make investigators believe the stiff displayed for their benefit was someone other than Holmes's longtime friend Ben Pitezel, there's no reason to assume he'd ever have been caught!

Fifty years later, it was the residents of Paris who'd be nauseated by the antics of a doctor who'd chosen to turn his skills to a particularly sadistic use. Dr Marcel Petiot caught the attention of his near neighbors when a pall of oily black smoke spilled out of his chimney. The stench so frightened the area's quiet residents that they wasted no time calling the police.

After breaking into Petiot's home, the shocked gendarmes staggered back out with tales of body parts stacked around a furnace already chocked full of burning corpses. The makeshift crematorium would eventually give up the remains of dozens of individuals!

Like Holmes, however, Petiot had the serial killer's smooth control of whatever situation he found himself in. It was 1944. The Resistance claimed small sections of Paris where they fought viciously to oust the turncoats who made a pathetic living carrying information to the Nazis. Claiming hero status for himself, Petiot insisted he'd been approached by a Resistance cell years before, that the bodies sizzling in his basement were the garbage the Resistance had asked him to dispose of and that, far from being a serial killer, he was repulsed by the entire situation, which was why the bodies had piled up. He'd had to work himself up to destroying even the remains of these foul invaders.

Nothing could have been farther from the truth.

Though police appeared to buy the story, they watched him covertly for several months, noting who he talked to and who talked to him. It didn't take long to realize that Petiot was being contacted by an inordinate number of German and French Jews – people who seldom turned up anywhere again.

Like Holmes, Petiot wasn't just a sadistic murderer, he was plain greedy! Posing as a member of the Resistance who could get Jews safely out of the country, he met his unsuspecting victims in remote locations, accepted their gratitude, brought them back to his house where he proceeded to 'innoculate' them against foreign diseases that the emigrants must be wary of, then left them locked in special rooms in the basement. It didn't take long for the refugees to realize that no simple innoculation could cause the violent, frothing death throes that would follow.

Petiot, after watching their agony as the strychnine he injected worked through their bodies, and their stunned realization that they'd been betrayed, would rob them of whatever wealth they'd been hoping to take to the New World with them, and tossed them into the furnace. A million pounds and an unknown number of victims later, Petiot died on the guillotine – an end some thought too bloody swift and relatively painless.

The killer nurses walk the fine line dividing serial killers from the plain, everyday, garden variety of killer. According to the FBI, serial killers are defined not only by the fact that they kill with 'three or more separate events with an emotional cooling-off period between homicides, each murder taking place at a different location', but by the sexual-sadism aspect of the crime. For some, 'serial killing' and 'lust killings' are interchangeable terms. Women are usually excluded from the 'serial killer' moniker because although they kill often, at different locations, with time between each event, they don't sexually assault or sadistically torture their victims. Without the sado-sexual angle, dozens of women – including an amazing number of nurses! – fall into the serial killer category.

The most famous is undoubtedly Anna Marie Hahn, a German immigrant to the United States who blithely went about healing the sick, unless she took a dislike to them, or their families, and decided to put her skills to an entirely different use. Nurse Hahn, whose patient list included an incredible number of wealthy widowers, had, by 1936, developed a real reputation for her loyalty and devotion to her patients, a

TO DATE, *MILLENNIUM* HASN'T REQUIRED HENRIKSEN TO FLOAT, SWIM, OR WEAR FUNNY UNIFORMS – EVEN IF HE GETS RAINED ON EVERY SECOND EPISODE

TESTIMONY TRIVIA 18

QUESTIONS

These should be dead simple for an observant fan.

1 To whom did Fabricant donate a kidney?
2 What did Catherine find in the refridgerator?
3 What was missing from Frank's filing cabinet?
4 Which judge presided at Fabricant's trial?
5 Where did Bletch's father bring him when he was a kid?

These two-pointers should prove a little more challenging!

6 What did Fabricant's 'rescuer' attack his guard with?
7 What verse did Fabricant send to Lucy Butler?
8 What was the second Biblical reference Frank found?
9 What name was put on the fake bracelet?
10 What's Frank's home phone number?

fact that's hard to reconcile with the eleven men she managed to poison in that same period. She's even suspected of making away with the odd relative who asked too many questions about Uncle So-and-So's sudden turn for the worse.

Nurse Grandy, an American, racked up 28 similar kills. The apparently-gentle governess known as Auntie Callie to her scores of charges was actually being comforted for the loss of her seventeenth young child when police arrived to arrest her. Whether they qualify as serial killers or just 'multi-murderers' probably doesn't matter much to the scores of victims whose trust they violated so completely.

Even those without a formal M.D. or R.N. after their names have been known to get in on the act. Take hospital orderly Donald Harvey as an example. Working across two states, at a number of facilities, Harvey, who preferred the effects of cyanide to almost anything else, reputedly killed 50 patients in just a few years. Harvey wasn't as exclusive as some of his fellow killers, however. Not only did he kill his patients, he took out their families, his own family, and a string of lovers, male and female.

Like the Dr Fabricant in 'Lamentation', the medical degrees Holmes and his ilk held weren't goals in themselves, but rather a means to put themselves in positions of respect where their crimes would be less credible, or where death, the companion they consistently sought out, could be more easily arranged. Just as there are pedophiles who become scout leaders, or swim coaches, or church youth group leaders, just to get legitimately close to their potential victims, there are dastardly doctors and nurses who delight in their scholarly study of corpses, who watch in fascination as they slowly take the life of a helpless patient, and even those who exalt in the opportunity to play 'hero' by 'saving' the very individuals they'd attempted to kill just moments ago.

One of these doctors, Charles Niles, who killed at least eighteen of his elderly patients, describes it: 'You can't imagine the power. The stupidity of these people! They come like lambs to the slaughter, putting their necks into your hands, making you their God. But, oooooh, the feeling. The complete control. The fading beat beneath your fingers, the connection, the eyes that look into yours, suddenly realizing their utter powerlessness … And they expect you to give that up? Let them go? I'd take the death penalty for one more like that.'

NOTEBOOK:

All That's Old is New Again

The 'truth is stranger than fiction' cliché is never more obviously true than in crime fiction, even crime fiction that incorporates psychic investigators and supernatural villians.

While the kidney transplant provided a number of necessary plotpoints for this episode, like a reason for Fabricant to be in a slightly less secure setting, it also harkens back to the epitome of serial killer mysteries – at least for buffs of the genre. Most historians pick Whitechapel's Jack the Ripper as the first modern serial killer, and many suspect that, like Fabricant, Jack was a man of science, a medical man, maybe even a doctor. One of the reasons the Jack-as-Doctor theory

ANSWERS

Remember to keep track of your score until the end.

Take a single point for each correct response.

1 His sister
2 A flashlight and a human kidney on a plate
3 His handgun
4 Judge Park
5 Mount Baker in Washington State's North Cascade Mountains

Collect two points for each correct answer below.

6 A fire extinguisher
7 Ezekiel 19:10
8 Judges 2:17
9 A. Nephric – anephric means 'without kidneys'
10 206-555-1130

YOUR SCORE:

remains so persuasive is that, in killing Catherine Eddowes, his second victim of the night, Jack the Ripper removed her left kidney with as deft a touch as any physician might have employed. It was yet one more example of the restrained fury he perpetuated on his victims, another example of the almost formal way he disembowelled his prey. Many had already been suggesting that the bodies resembled horrid parodies of medical school cadaver studies.

Like Fabricant's kidney, which turned up in the house of the man chasing him, Eddowes's missing organ ended up in the hands of George Lusk who led the Ripper investigation. His horror was no less than Catherine's – and the Ripper's attached message, with its return address of 'FROM HELL', 'Catch me when you can …' is as pertinent to this episode as it was a hundred years ago.

The very fact that Fabricant escaped from federal custody may seem shocking to modern audiences. Certainly, few killers of Fabricant's magnitude even get the opportunity. Still, some of the more famous killers, like Ted Bundy, have done just that – and more than once! Bundy's flights from his captors in Aspen, Colorado, rivaled most fiction for inventiveness. Claiming legal privileges because he was defending himself, Bundy managed to get himself a pass to the law library. Once inside, he simply jumped from a second-story window and legged it out across the campus grounds. You might think Bundy's little two-day vacation might have made his jailors more observant. Apparently not. The second time, Bundy escaped from, of all places, his own cell. After cutting a hole through the ceiling of the jail, he crawled through the floorspace, and out a side exit. This time, it would take the authorities months to track him and, during that time, Bundy would kill three more times.

Creating any character, even a shape-changing, probably-demonic, creature like the one in Frank's basement

WHAT EXACTLY GOES ON BEHIND THOSE EYES?

forces writers to imagine the depths of human depravity. Fortunately or unfortunately, depending on your viewpoint, there is little that a sane writer can come up with that hasn't already been tried by the real killers.

Even Lucy Butler's apparently bizarre behavior in marrying a psychopath like Ephraim Fabricant has its real-life parallels. Ed Gein, an ugly, loathsome, necrophiliac who liked to wear women's skins and pretend to be his own mother, would have been bald for years if he'd handed out all the locks of hair women asked of him. Jeffrey Dahmer, who was turned on by the sound of stomach gurglings and liked to eat his lovers, received six offers of marriage despite his brief prison career. The man who killed him has received death threats.

INCIDENTALS:

If the name 'Fabricant' seems elusively familiar, it's possible you're thinking of the very real-life mass murderer, Dr Valeri Fabrikant who, believing his paranoid delusions that his colleagues were stealing his work, that the university staff were 'out to get him' and that's why he was refused tenure, shot and killed four people at Concordia University in Montreal in addition to seriously injuring a fifth.

☐

INTERESTED IN AN ON-LINE WEDDING OF YOUR OWN?

A group called FECHA, the First Electronic Church of America, can handle all the details for you. Find them at

http://www.wsone.com/fecha/ed.html

and then toss the confetti!

CASE NUMBER: M-119-04-25-97

CASE FILE: **'Powers, Principalities, Thrones and Dominions'**

CASE SYNOPSIS:

Frank Black's return to work is clouded by doubt and confusion when, in addition to alarmingly realistic dreams, he finds himself faced with a growing, if baseless, conviction that a series of apparently Satanic killings is connected to the death of his friend, Robert Bletcher.

KEY CITATION:

'I cut a detective's neck in Seattle.
I left him hanging on a basement wall.
Bletcher. Bob Bletcher was his name.
I don't know why, but, it's been
bothering me.'

MARTIN

VITAL STATISTICS:

Original US Airdate:	04/25/97
Production Number:	4C118
Written by:	Ted Mann
Directed by:	Harold Rosenthal

Guest Cast:

Terry O'Quinn	Peter Watts
Stephen James Lang	Detective Giebelhouse
Robin Gammell	Mike Atkins
Bonnie Hay	Assistant DA Mills
Richard Cox	Al Pepper
Alf Humphreys	Damon Rummer
Allan Franz	Medical Examiner Anderson
Judith Maxie	Judge Myers
Dean P Gibson	Phil Brice
Guy Fauchon	Martin
Robert Moloney	Uniformed Cop Adams
Rodney Eastman	Sam
LyonGerry	Nairn
Terry King	Mike
Marya Delver	Nanny Annie

Death Toll:	2 males, bled to death, ritual murder
	1 female, throat slit
	1 male, 'natural causes'

CASE HISTORY:

THE ANGELS AMONG US

This episode, whose name 'Powers, Principalities, Thrones and Dominions' urges us to look beyond the merely material, poses more questions than it answers. What exactly was Al Pepper: just a sleaze-ball

LANCE HENRIKSEN IN 'STONE COLD'

lawyer who hires the best investigators, or an agent of some other, less-worldly, authority? And Samiel? A 90s angel, as his name implies, with a hip haircut and good patter?

That Frank Black believed he was dealing with something highly unusual goes without saying. After all, it was Frank who picked up the so-called murder weapon only to discover the hammer had never fallen, that the shell was still snugly secured in the chamber. It was Frank who saw a bolt of energy slam into Al Pepper, Frank who, even before the case took its more bizarre turns, believed that the evil here was, in some way, related to the evil perpetrated in his own basement.

If the title gives viewers some clue, that's all it is, a clue, one that doesn't answer many questions if the 'angels' it alludes to are assumed to be nothing more than the cherubic images adorning a new wave of coffee cups, calendars and jewellery. If, however, the title is taken in its Biblical, and even pre-Biblical, connotations, a few more hints may be waiting.

Christianity has been called the 'bastardized religion' by theologic historians, and with good cause. Despite claiming to be based strictly on the Bible and Christian interpretation of the scriptures, Christianity does, in fact, continue to incorporate the myths and folktales that preceded it. It's no surprise then that Christian festivals fall on the dates of earlier pagan rites, or that Christmas trees and Easter eggs, neither to be found in any Bible, have become part of Christianity's modern expression. It was that sort of early-ecumenical thinking that allowed a new religion to be accepted first as an alternative to local practices, then, gradually, as a replacement for the old ways. Still, such inclusions can make it difficult to determine which of the many pretty legends is actually canonical and which have become traditional simply because assimilation was easier, smoother, than outright insurrection.

Such is certainly true in the case of angels. Though angels are mentioned through the Christian Bible, the strict hierarchies of angelic power and responsibility which survive today could never have been determined from the scant Biblical passages devoted to them! An analogy would be building a space shuttle from viewing, just once, the flight of a child's paper dart!

Still, one of the wonders of a living religion is that it supposedly grows, leaving room for new discoveries and new understandings. Given that, and the fact that most religions have oral histories and traditions in addition to their formal texts, the tales of angels certainly present an intriguing peek into the oft-ignored world of Christian, Judaic, and Islamic mysticism.

In fact, it's entirely possible that the creatures which Christians have embraced with such affection in the 1990s may be one of the very few things all three of those faiths have been able to agree on in the last couple of millennia! Though there was, of course, an acknowledgement among Christians that the 'angels' of the Bible did exist, in some heavenly sphere, it was Christianity's shoulder-rubbing with its religious cousins, not to mention the Zoroastrians who predate Christianity in the Middle East, that fixed the angels into the formal hierarchy we have today.

Remember the Christmas carol line, 'Sing choirs of angels!'? According to modern belief, there are actually nine choirs, each composed of a particular sort of angel with its own powers and functions, with each choir either superior to or subordinate to each of the remaining eight. The first order, those closest to God, include the Seraphim, Cherubim, and the Thrones.

Seraphim were revealed to Isaiah, an Old Testament prophet, as towering creatures of consuming flame. The word 'seraphim' itself comes from the Hebrew for 'flaming'. Almost too awe-inspiring even to look on, they may number 4, 7, 12, or 70, depending on the source. All references, however, seem to agree that the seraphim have not two, but six wings! The first set of two covers the seraphim's face, the second set covers his feet rather like the Roman messenger god Mercury, and the last set conforms to the usual position assumed by modern audiences. Psalm 103:4 recalls, 'Who maketh his angels spirits; his ministers a flaming fire.' These

wonderous creations stand before God's seat, constantly worshipping, constantly at one with their master.

The next order, the Cherubim, are often depicted on cards and placemats as rather pudgy children supported by wings that defy physics as well as theology. In biblical terms, however, they're the embodiment of God's wisdom. In Hebrew, 'cherubim' means 'great understanding' and these angels are traditionally described as 'glowing' and 'radiant' in their knowledge of God. Where the seraphim resemble flames, the cherubim throw out light like small suns.

The Thrones, the last of the Trinity devoted to the contemplation of God Himself, are starker, sterner creatures representing justice. In reality, Thrones are only described in Biblical passages, never named. It was St Dionysius the Areopagite who gave them their odd name after considering Psalm 9:4, 'Thou hast sat upon a throne, O Thou that judgest righteousness.' It was as a permanent manifestation of that aspect of God that the Thrones were named, and it's from this heavenly source that kings claim their Divine Right to rule.

The next Trinity of Angels, those responsible for the creations of God, consist of the Dominions, the Virtues and the Powers.

The Dominions, sometimes called Dominations, are noteworthy for their complete lack of servile fear which allows them to lead other angels. It's from these angels that God's 'anointed Kings' have learned earthly wisdom, to subdue base passions and desires that could interfere with the delivery of God's justice.

The Virtues have little to do with the modern-day interpretation of the word which tends to conjure up ideals like Faith, Hope, and Charity. The Virtues real 'virtue' is strength – the strength to perform miracles or endow deserving humans with the same power. The word 'strength' when applied to the Virtues is better associated with the ability to will the impossible into being than with lifting tractor trailers. Healing the sick, resurrecting the dead, or foretelling the future are all acts within the realm of influence governed by the Virtues.

The Powers fulfill a very specific function. Given the 'power' to turn aside temptation, the Powers conspire to restrain the devil, to temper the power of demons, and pro-

tect the weak who'd normally be their targets. Their goal is to provide a level playing field for mortals hoping to achieve Heaven by helping their weaker cousins to avoid temptation and vice. Whether by influencing the mortals in their charge, or by direct confrontation with the devil and his demons, it's the Powers that supposedly stand between us and our worst natures.

The last Trinity of Angels, those who are most likely to appear to humans, and who have dominion over the things of man, includes the Principalities, the Archangels, and the Angels themselves, the supernatural beings who gave their name to all the rest.

Principalities, not surprisingly, are the overseers of groups, the management of everything from universes to kingdoms, from races to families being their primary concern. It's through the offices of the principalities that particular individuals come to govern – and to serve the needs of those they govern. Though all the angels are said to teach God's purpose to his people, the Principalities teach individuals to find their assigned role and to develop the skills needed to fulfill that

ANGEL OR DEMON? LOOKS LIKE FRANK ISN'T SURE EITHER!

TESTIMONY TRIVIA 19

QUESTIONS

These are the easy ones!

1 What Group member turned up unexpectedly at the crime scene?
2 Who did Frank dream was in his living room?
3 What did Martin attempt to cut his throat with?
4 What did Pepper technically die from six months prior?
5 Where did Martin kill the babysitter?

Give these a bit more thought.

6 What Greek word gave Frank and the others pause for thought?
7 How did Giebelhouse describe Martin?
8 What did Martin die of?
9 Name any two of the people Frank recognized in the market.
10 Who killed Pepper?

role. Finally, like administrators, the Principalities govern the lower angels, ensuring that they fulfill their own Divine Orders.

The Archangels, the only angels known to have Biblical names, have a closer relationship with humanity than the other, higher, orders. Portrayed as heralds, the archangels reveal prophecies, carrying the news of great events like the Annunciation. On a spiritual level, they bring knowledge of God and his intentions directly to individuals and nations. It was the Archangels who spoke to John the Baptist and Mary.

Perhaps because of their more direct association with people, the Archangels have a number of well-defined individuals among their ranks. The Archangel Michael, for example, is believed to have led God's armies against the Devil, driving him out of heaven. That four of the Archangels, Michael, Rafael, Gabriel, and Uriel, are often portrayed as the four elements, the cardinal points of the compass, or any other grouping of four, may be based more in earlier Eastern philosophies than Christianity. The Archangels, both the four mentioned here and others, figure in the legends of Persia (now Iran) going back centuries before Christianity came to the area. Likewise, Kabbalistic tradition includes the existence of angels and the four Archangels have their contemporaries there as well.

The last choir, the lowest, are the angels themselves, those supernatural beings who are the closest to humanity.

According to a common Eastern belief, an angel is assigned to every human being at the time of their conception, an idea that's resulted in the Western notion of a Guardian Angel, and that this Guardian acts much like an external conscience, guiding and teaching with little nudges instead of the Archangels' grander revelations. Of course, under special circumstances, the Biblical angels appeared to a number of people, among them the prophet Daniel.

You'd almost think, with all the hope and enlightenment intrinsic to the nine choirs of angels, that there'd be no opportunity for evil to sneak its way into the world. Almost. Religion, like science, however, tends to be a symmetrical thing. Just as any discussion of angels assumes that these supernatural beings exist in a spiritual reality that only rarely comes into contact with our material world, a duality, it's also assumed that, first of all, there are evil equivalents to all the choirs and that the two are constantly engaged in some struggle for control of both the spiritual and physical realms. The image of the Devil as a fallen angel is, Biblically correct or not, fixed in Christian minds. It's within this framework that the episode 'Powers, Principalities, Thrones and Dominions' begins to tickle our collective understanding of good and evil.

If there were indeed ranks, or choirs, of fallen angels, all serving a common master, all struggling for the control of a physical world, then Lucy Butler, Al Pepper, Martin, even the Judge who called himself Legion and the man from the series première, the one with a taste for stuffing young men into microwave ovens, can be seen as aspects, or agents, of the same power, the same evil.

In 'Lamentations', Robert Bletcher sees a woman on the stairs; Catherine sees a man. Angels, in all their heavenly forms, have traditionally been portrayed as androgynous beings, most lacking a physical body of any sort unless they were compelled to communicate with humanity. If Frank's ultimate adversary is indeed a devil in command of choirs of demons, then his perceptions in the market, of a montage of changing faces, the numerous voices heard over the phone, and Peter's doubts about what he saw outside a second-story window begin to gain some sense of logic.

WILL THE YELLOW
HOUSE EVER SEEM
THIS SECURE AGAIN?

Then, of course, there's Samiel, the being Frank can't quite explain to Peter, who appears and disappears almost at will, and who, according to Frank's observation, strikes with fire instead of bullets. If the *Millennium* universe includes beings like angels – and their demonic opposite numbers – and if it also follows the traditional belief that only certain people have the facility to see where the physical and spiritual worlds merge, there's nothing to exclude a Samiel or to exclude Frank's unusual visions. Christian history, as opposed to theology, actually includes an archangel Sam-iel, brother to Raf-iel, Ur-iel, Gabr-iel and Mik-iel as they're known in the East and, in that tradition, Sam-iel is 'the leveler', the one who lends his power to the mismatched struggle between demons and humanity. That the Anglicized version, Sammael, appears in modern Bibles as a high-ranking angel as well as an equally highly-placed demon, capable of both taking human life and destroying lesser supernatural beings, only seems to solidify this view of the world *Millennium* is slowly creating.

If Carter's intention was to present a scenario that 'really gets down to the basics, that's Light against the Darkness', he's certainly begun assembling a supernatural cast capable of doing just that.

NOTEBOOK:

The Satanic Myth

'The ritual elements at the murder scene were drawn from a wide variety of mystic traditions. Stage-dressing. The work of a schizoid fantasist lacking any spiritual seriousness.'

FRANK BLACK

In 1992, the FBI completed a report on its investigations into claims that a Satanic cult was methodically murdering people across the United States. Three years ago, the La Fontaine report presented the results of its own investigation into similar claims in the United Kingdom. Since 1980, some $200m has been spent by various other levels of government and law enforcement, all looking for some sign that ritual Satanic murders were more than a figment of someone's overactive imagination.

What did they collectively find as a result of all these studies and reports?

Nothing.

Zip, nada, zilch.

Sure, there were some interesting cases to look into, but, precious little evidence of any type to support even the suggestion of Satanism at work. One such case involved a child found torn to pieces in June 1996, just outside Ottawa, Canada. Even before the pathology and autopsy reports could be typed, the media was suggesting something vaguely sinister. When the reports were a bit longer than usual coming in, the level of hysteria rose and, by nightfall, rumors of Satanic abuse were flying. Almost no one reported the investigator's final findings, that the child had been abandoned by its mother, died, and been subject to considerable animal predation. Despite the fact that a baby is found almost weekly in American dumpsters, the general public never did fully accept that this was just another case of child abandonment in a slightly unusual locale.

Those who insist that Satanic ritual murders exist outside the fictional worlds of television, books, and films, point to characters like Richard Ramirez, who flashed an inverted pentagram on his palm at jurors during his trial, as proof of Satanic killings. The fact that Ramirez, also known as The Night Stalker, frequently insisted his victims swear their allegiance to Satan before killing or raping them, and that he liked to paint what he believed were Satanic symbols around the homes of his targets, only solidified the myth in some people's minds.

The problem, actually two problems, is that Ramirez worked alone and had no idea what Satanic practices might entail! The whole notion of a nationwide conspiracy falls apart rather quickly when the killings are the work of a single madman. Like the 'evidence' Peter Watts found, with Egyptian myths mixed in with a heavy dose of Crowley, the staging at Ramirez's crime scenes never made much sense.

Another famous murderer who claimed to be involved in a Satanic cult was David Berkowitz, the Son of Sam. Then again, he also claimed to receive demonic instructions from his neighbor's dog! It should also be noted that all these outrageous claims stopped rather abruptly after the court determined he just wasn't crazy enough to get off on an insanity plea. When he didn't need to be crazy, he didn't need to have a personal relationship with Satan either.

In over a decade of investigation, absolutely no hard evidence of a Satanic conspiracy has been turned up.

What about the 'soft' evidence then? The recollection of dozens of women, some made famous by publication as non-fiction books? Frankly, to date, not one has held up to investigation. In one rather notorious case, the incidents claimed in the book couldn't have happened as related. The 'victim', who claimed to have been entangled in a Satanic cult while at summer camp had never even gotten on the bus. She was the only one in her church group to miss the trip altogether! She was left at home because she had mumps, a fact any number of people, including her doctor and parents, verified within a week of the book's publication!

Of course, not every person claiming to be a victim of Satanic abuse is a deliberate liar hoping to cop a few bucks from a quickie book sale. Some of these people seem entirely sincere in their beliefs and their efforts to ensure no one else suffers a similiar fate, but, well, hundreds of people each year also claim to be abducted by aliens.

Who's spending $200m to check that out?

No one.

INCIDENTALS:

The market where Frank Black chases the morphing Al Pepper is actually a well-known health food store in the neighborhood and, when it's not being used as a set for *Millennium*, Megan Gallagher is known to pick up her groceries there.

☐

'The name carries some notoriety in certain circles.' It certainly does if Pepper is referring to Aleister Crowley!

Crowley, who preferred being referred to as 'The Beast 666', was a British Satanist who spent much of his life reviling Christianity. Though he claimed to traffic in 'magick', he never proved that point in public. Instead, he used most of his charm and charisma to separate foolish women from their money!

SO MUCH FOR FRANK'S ATTEMPT AT EARLY INTERVENTION

CASE FILE: 'Broken World'

CASE SYNOPSIS:

A string of horse mutilations brings Frank Black to North Dakota in the hope that his intervention can stop the genesis of yet another serial killer. When contact is made, however, it becomes evident that the budding killer is already deep in the grips of his escalating fantasy and Frank must help a sceptical local law enforcement agency track a killer they can't even recognize yet.

KEY CITATION:

'His only source for feeling alive is his urge
for sexual pleasure. His paraphilia has now
defined it. It intoxicates and terrifies him.
He's standing at an abyss and
he's hesitating.'

FRANK BLACK

VITAL STATISTICS:

Original US Airdate:	05/02/97
Production Number:	4C119
Written by:	Robert Moresco
	Patrick Harbinson
Directed by:	Winrich Kolbe

Guest Cast:

Terry O'Quinn	Peter Watts
John Dennis Johnston	Sheriff Falkner
Michael Tayles	Deputy Billy
J B Bivens	The First Deputy
Van Quattro	Killer Willi Borgsen
Ingrid Kavelaars	Sally Dumont
Donnelly Rhodes	Peter Dumont
Sue Fuller	Mary Ann
Jo Anderson	Claudia Vaughan
Tom Bougers	Tom
P Adrien Dorval	Fatso

Death Toll:	1 male, kicked/stabbed to death
	1 male, trampled
	1 female, butchered

CASE HISTORY:

THE TRIAD: SIGNS OF SERIAL KILLER

'My work normally begins with dead bodies,
multiples of dead bodies. I came here because
I think we have a chance to stop this killing before
it starts. We're witnessing the birth of a
psychosexual killer.'

FRANK BLACK

That, in a nutshell, is the starting position of every homicide detective, whether they work for a small local police department, or walk the halls of the Washington Bureau of the FBI. If serial killers were born with a big 'SK' tattooed to their foreheads, cops and special agents could just cruise the nurseries and save future generations a whole lot of effort and aggravation – not to mention lives. Unfortunately, while serial killers sometimes like to carve symbols into their bodies, they don't come into the world that way, which means an awful lot of cops and psychologists spend considerable portions of their lives trying to find some other, more subtle way of determining which of the kids in any random kindergarten class is likely to grow into a ravenous sado-sexual killer.

Needless to say, a number of theories have been proposed and tossed out over the years. As with most situations that occur outside the confines of a lab, there are always exceptions to disprove the latest postulations. Take the XYY chromosome theory that was popular in the 1960s. It stated that because some serial killers had this extra 'male' chromosome, it made them more aggressive, more animalistic. Richard Speck, who slaughtered eight young student nurses in Chicago, made the XYY Chromosomal Theory his defence – only to discover the lab had buggered the results and he didn't even have this extra chromosome!

So-called 'negative parenting', which includes everything from fathers wandering about naked in front of impressionable young serial killers, to mothers who thrust broomsticks up their sons' anuses on a regular basis, to yet other parents of both sexes who sent their sons to school in ringlets and dresses, was the next theory. Certainly, few serial killers have the sort of childhood we'd want for ourselves, and parental abuse probably didn't do much for Charlie Manson or Albert Fish, but literally thousands of children survive abusive parents, in fact not only survive but develop a deep and abiding intolerance for violence. And, if environment was the determining factor, how to explain monsters like Ted Bundy or Paul Bernardo who came from run-of-the-mill middle-class homes?

HMMMM? If Frank and Peter had really believed the guy used the phone and tossed his paper in the corner, then why were both men handling the paper instead of bagging it as evidence and sending it along to be dusted?

Clearly the stages in the development of a serial killer are as elusive as the stages in the development of a genius. Without a checklist of causes, psychologists and cops turn to symptoms to help them identify serial killers and, in that category, there does seem to be something of a pattern available, something called the Triad. The Triad symptoms of fire-starting, enuresis, and sadism, especially towards animals, repeat over and over again among the worst of the multi-murderers.

Henry Lee Lucas took considerable pleasure in relating the most disgusting aspects of his life to a number of investigators and psychologists after his jail-house religious conversion. He grinned continuously while describing orgies that included his thirteen-year-old self, his fifteen-year-old half brother, and a variety of small, furry animals. The two tortured and sexually assaulted cats, puppies, a neighbor's pet rabbit, anything they could get their hands on. Lucas continued to enjoy bestiality and animal torture well into his twenties, by which time he'd already killed several women. Lucas had no inhibitions during his interviews. 'Did I piss the bed? Yeah. And I know what you want to know next, same thing

TESTIMONY TRIVIA 20

QUESTIONS

These are the easy ones.

1 What was the name of the local paper?
2 What did the killer use on Sally, some pigs and a pig farmer?
3 What was written in blood in the stall?
4 What was found in the straw of a horse stall?
5 Where did the killer work?

These should make you really think!

6 How many horse attacks occurred prior to Frank's arrival?
7 What was the name of Sally's horse?
8 What was the nickname given to the 800 number line?
9 What was collected on the farm where the killer grew up?
10 From what work did the vet's poster phrase come?

everyone wants to know, when did I stop. After I killed my first woman, I was fourteen. I didn't have that problem no more after that.' Though Lucas didn't burn down any buildings, as his partner Ottis Toole did quite early in life, he started any number of smaller fires, often combining them with his animal torture routines.

Peter Kürten, also known as the Monster of Düsseldorf, followed an almost identical pattern. He fell under the early sway of an older man on his street, the local dog-catcher, who indoctrinated young Peter in the fun and laughs to be had with a bunch of helpless animals. Between torture and masturbation and animal sodomy, it's no small wonder Peter Kürten's view of adult sexual relations was warped. Instead of girlfriends, Peter Kürten just went looking for bigger animals. He openly confessed to reaching the ultimate in sexual satiation while simultaneously raping and stabbing a pig to death. Kürten's interests turned to women only after exploring the thrills in capturing, torturing and sexually assailing dogs, cats, pigs, goats and sheep in the crucial teen years between thirteen and fifteen. In 1929, Kürten, in a sadistic rage, fell on

a sleeping swan in Hoftgarten, a Düsseldorf public park, ripped off its head and drank the blood spurting from its neck as he fantasized about his next human kill. For him, sex, sadism and animal torture were a tangled psychological mess that no fiction writer could hope to explain or top.

Maybe it was a natural progression considering his early choice of 'dates', but Kürten also took great pleasure in masturbating while watching a barn he'd just torched go up in flames. The screams of burning animals only increased his high. By his own admittedly confused estimates, he burned at least eleven buildings to the ground, and attempted a dozen more. Fire, like his total physical domination of his victims both human and otherwise, expressed another aspect of his need for control. The fact that he couldn't make it through the night without wetting his bed until he was well into his twenties, however, proved just how tenuous his 'control' actually was.

Far from isolated cases, Lucas and Kürten are merely representative samples of the numerous serial killers who never grew up enough to stop pulling wings off flies, who took delight in imposing terror and pain on their victims before imposing the ultimate control, death.

Dahmer, who always looked so nice and neat, didn't just catch frogs like every other little boy, he nailed them to trees, opened their abdomens and watched their body functions until life drained away. Anyone watching a boy with a pole on a riverbank or pond side, especially a quiet, distant, young boy would assume he'd simply fallen under the magic of a day spent trying to outwit a fish.

Not Dahmer.

No, the fishing itself was only a means to an end, it was the gutting of his catch that Dahmer was anticipating! Long after he was captured and convicted on fifteen counts of murder, neighbors would whisper of the afternoon when their kids had discovered a dog's head mounted on a stick and stuck in the ground.

While most serial killers move on from animal torture and murder to human targets, where they often continue to practice the skills they perfected on unfortunate cats and dogs, Pater Groll of Austria is one of the few known to keep up his childhood 'habit' well into adulthood. When a group of villagers dragged him from his home on the suspicion that his dates weren't just disappearing after going out with him, they were as disgusted by the animal carnage they found as the clear evidence that four of the village's young women had died in his house.

Inside the otherwise tidy home, Pater Groll maintained a cellar that would have put the Tower of London to shame. A

DIFFERENT PROJECT,
DIFFERENT DOG,
SAME CHARM

bottomless cage rested atop a sheet of metal which, in turn, rested over half a piece of metal culvert piping just deep enough to hold a few shovelfuls of hot coals. When not entertaining his short-lived girlfriends, Pater Groll would lock some unsuspecting creature, usually a cat, inside the cage, toss coals under the metal sheet and watch the doomed animal's attempts to keep all its feet off the increasingly hot 'floor'. From Groll's own admissions, it could take as much as three hours for the poor animal to die, 'depending on how careful I was with the coals.'

A miniature 'rack' still contained the drying remains of an eviscerated lamb from which Groll 'removed the organs one by one, to see how much of it could be outside before it got into real trouble'. Real trouble? Perhaps that's a term he reserved for the poor animals they found stumbling about in the barn out back.

The dun-colored mare shivering in a stall that hadn't seen a shovel in months couldn't blink in the light coming through the stable door – it had no eyelids and the pus clinging to its cheeks provided mute evidence that it couldn't have seen its rescuers anyway. What its rescuers saw sent grown men back outside to retch weakly in the mud. The mare's skin had been systematically flayed from its back in inch-wide strips leaving crusty streaks where an inadequate diet and lack of water made it practically impossible for the poor brute to heal even normal damage, much less this carnage. Ham-strung and blind, with dozens of nicks around its throat indicating Groll had likely been bleeding it for several months to satisfy his self-proclaimed blood-lust, the weakened horse couldn't even avoid its captor.

Confronted with his sadism, Groll shrugged the incident off with the comment, 'If the girls had been more entertaining, I wouldn't have had to do that too. I'll miss the horse, she was a good horse.'

NOTEBOOK:

Like Phases of the Moon

Just how did Frank know what his budding serial killer was experiencing? What he was feeling and thinking? Aside from Frank's more unique talents, his writers could draw on the accumulated knowledge of hundreds of criminal investigators, including psychologists, who've spent thousands of man-hours interviewing and assessing the behavior of serial killers. From those often-harrowing investigations has come a model of serial killer activity that's proven itself so often as to become an accepted standard, even amid the chaotic vagaries of hundreds of serial killers – The Seven-Step Profile.

Step One: The Aura Phase: Serial killers aren't like mass murderers who just 'snap'. The serial killer indulges in a rich fantasy life, often for decades before trying to act out the bizarre images in his head. This stage of development intensifies, however, until the killer must find some way to merge his fantasy and real worlds.

Step Two: The Troll Phase: Once he's decided he can no longer be satisfied with his fantasy, the killer must take some action to put himself in the same proximity as his intended victims. This might be an obvious action, like hanging in a red-light district until a prostitute wanders off on her own for a few moments. It might mean lurking in the shrubbery next to a playground. It might even mean staying at home! John Wilkers had never seen his mailman before 26 August, 1943, when he not only met him, but killed him. Wilkers falsely believed his mailman was having an affair with his wife, and, after allowing himself to fantasize about killing the man, the normally punctual Wilkers stayed home and waited for the unfortunate postal carrier to come to him. Wilkers would go on to track down his wife's butcher, the young boy who clipped the grass and hedges on Saturdays, a plumber, the plumber's assistant, and a number of other people who had casual contact with his wife, but, for his first kill, he 'trolled' at home.

Step Three: The Wooing Phase: It's not always easy to get a victim to co-operate. Children, for example, who used to be so innocent, now scream their heads off if strangers approach them with a lollipop. Women are less likely to accept rides than they used to be. Even men are more inclined to call Roadside Assistance than be caught on the side of the road, alone, with a car that won't move. So begins the wooing stage, the stage when a killer convinces his victim that he means them no harm. In Los Angeles, a rash of rape-murders were tied to two men who, using fake IDs and uniforms, convinced their victims that they were police officers and that there might be some prowler in their home. Then again, there are those killers who actually enjoy this phase of the chase, for whom the luring of their victims is yet another way to prove to themselves that they are superior in some way to those they hunt. In each case, whether from choice or necessity, killers must either gain quick, complete control of their victim, or gain their confidence to a degree that the killer can expect to be able to lure them into their control in a reasonable amount of time.

Step Four: The Capture: The moment when victims realize their utter helplessness is, for many killers, the aim of all that has gone before. Now, with the victim secured, they can play out all their sick games and imaginings. Death, while often unavoidable, isn't always the goal. If the victim dies, the killer must start all over again. Even for those whose biggest thrill, the kill, is yet to come, this singular moment is a reward in itself, the beginning of a high.

Step Five: The Kill: Killers, almost by definition, intend to kill. For some, the death of their captured victim is a let-down, the moment when they can no longer exert their total control, no longer inflict pain and terror. For others, though, the death throes of their chosen target are like a sexual climax – many killers ejaculate just as the light fades from their victim's eyes or just as their bodies fall limp.

Step Six: The Transition: While still high from their success, most killers will find some way to extend their delight, their pleasure, in their kill. Some spend the moments immediately after a kill collecting 'trophies' of one sort or another, under-wear, body parts, and jewellery are common trophies, any-thing that will help them relive this moment in later fantasies. Other killers, especially those who enjoy the sadism of torture more than the death throes, however, are markedly angry at this stage, feeling almost cheated of their fun by the victim who dared die. Transition for these killers is frequently marked by violent assaults against the dead body. Post-mortem hack-ing and slashing and even dismemberment and sex staged with a view to leaving the body in as degrading a position as possible, can all become part of the mix.

Step Seven: Let-Down: Even if everything has gone perfectly from the killer's point of view, meaning that he found and successfully lured the victim of his dreams, and that he tortured or murdered at his leisure, satisfying all his sick desires as fully as possible, there must still be the let-down. As murder so often replaces normal sexual gratification for serial killers, this period can be compared to the normal person's post-sex lethargy. For serial killers, who seem to live at the extremes of emotion, this lull, the cooling-off period, can become so intense they actually develop a condition known as post-homicidal depression!

To relieve this malaise, killers typically follow one of three courses.

One: kill again. As the murderer begins to indulge new fantasies, to picture ways of repeating or even exceeding the pleasure of his last kill, he eases away from Step Seven and back to the Aura stage, ready to kill yet again.

Two: suicide. Though some killers, like the Lipstick Killer, expressed remorse for their crimes even before being caught, most killers never do develop any concern for the victims or their families. It isn't horror at their own actions that leads such men to suicide but their depression, the let-down of the fantasy, or the growth of a new fantasy, namely to discover what it's like from the victim's view, that will occasionally result in a killer killing himself.

And the last option, the one taken least often, is, of course, to stop killing. Only one killer is on record as having made a decision not to kill again. He's Hans Rupeth, formerly of South Africa, who, on his deathbed, confessed to having been the one to kill his sister, thus solving a case that had puzzled police for three decades. Until then, the police would have categorically denied even the possibility of Hans's involvement. When asked why he'd stopped, he replied, 'It really wasn't all it was cracked up to be.'

ANSWERS

Take a single point for each correct answer.

1 *The Echo*
2 An electric cattle prod
3 'Thank You'
4 Semen
5 At a slaughterhouse

Two points for each of these.

6 21
7 Phaethon
8 1-800-PONY-RIDE
9 Pregnant mare's urine
10 Blake's 'Augeries of Innocence'

YOUR SCORE:

MAYBE CATHERINE IS WONDERING WHY SHE BARELY GOT TO SEE HER HUSBAND IN THE SECOND HALF OF THE SEASON?

INCIDENTALS:

Not surprisingly, this episode was originally titled 'Equus'.

□

GUEST FILMOGRAPHY:
JO ANDERSON (VETERINARY
DOCTOR, CLAUDIA VAUGHAN)

Daylight (1996) – Boom
Menendez: A Killing in Beverly Hills (1994)
– Pam Bozanich
Season of Change (1994) – Martha Parker
Sisters (1994–1996) – Dr Charlotte Bennett
Northern Exposure (1992) – Roslyn
Dead Again (1991) – Sister Madeleine/Starlet
JFK (1991) – Julia Ann Mercer
Decoration Day (1990) – Loreen Wendell
Dream Street (1989) – Marianne McKinney
Columbo: Uneasy Lies the Crown (1989)
– Mrs Lydia Corman
Prime Target (1989) – McGuire
I Saw What You Did (1988) – Robyn
Miles From Home (1988) – Farmer's Wife
Beauty and the Beast (1987) – Diana Bennett
Suspicion (1987) – Secretary
Jamaica Inn (1985) – Prisoner's Woman

CASE FILE: 'Maranatha'

CASE SYNOPSIS:

A Russian emigre community closes in on itself just when New York police most need local help in finding a serial killer with a very professional MO. A St Petersburg cop, supposedly in the country to help, seriously undermines the case by refusing to admit the signs Frank finds linking the killing to an apocalyptic Russian legend are anything more than 'boogeymen'.

KEY CITATION:

'Frank, Russia is crazy now. Old superstitions coming back. Priests and tea-readers preying on people's fears better than the communists ever did. See, to a Russian, everything must be magic. It's not enough that a man commits these murders. No, it must be "Yaponchik walks the earth". Ooooh. True evil.'

YURA SUROVA

VITAL STATISTICS:

Original US Airdate:	05/09/97
Production Number:	4C120
Written by:	Chip Johannessen
Directed by:	Peter Markle

Guest Cast:

Terry O'Quinn	Peter Watts
Bill Nunn	Lt McCormick
Vladimir Moskovchenko	Elder Evgenii Alexandrovitch
Dmitri Boudrine	Andrei Petrovich Melnikov
Boris Krutonog	Yura Surova
Mateev Levani Outchaneichvili	Yaponchik
Beverly Pales	The Torch Singer
Michael Aniol	The Priest
Bill Croft	Broadface
Brian Downey	The Medical Examiner
Michael Cram	The Paramedic
Roger Haskett	The E.R. Doctor

Death Toll:	Unknown males and females, nuclear explosion
	5 male, shotgun blast
	1 female, shotgun blast

CASE HISTORY:

FROM THE HEADLINES

In creating 'Maranatha', *Millennium*'s writers could build their apocalyptic visionary on an already well-established model. The Russian mob, once

considered a rather new and upstart group of opportunists flourishing in the chaos between the fall of the old regime and the building of a new style of government and law enforcement, is now recognized as having been an integral part of Russian society since before the Bolshevik Revolution. A hundred years of history is nothing to sneeze at in any country, and the extrapolation, that a 'secret society' might harbor secret plans and even knowledge, isn't so great a stretch. The Masons and other groups, both religious and secular, have long been accused of guarding – and, in the process, hiding – esoteric knowledge and end-time prophecy.

That the Russian version of a mob exists in New York City is also something of a given considering the recent arrest of Vyacheslav Kirillovich Ivankov, the latest 'Yaponchik'. Literally translated as 'the little Jap', fifty-five-year-old Ivankov did have something of an Oriental cast to his features, but most Russians believe the nickname, a matter of considerable thought amongst the highly organized hierarchy of *vor v zakone*, the 'thieves who profess the code', was a deliberate attempt to cover himself in the honor accorded a string of powerful Russian dons all named 'Yaponchik'. So,

THE SYMBOLISM IS CLEAR, THE EMOTION RAW IN 'MARANATHA'

in a practical sense, the history behind *Millennium*'s Yaponchik does have some basis in fact.

Could the Yaponchik in 'Maranatha' have organized the accident at Chernobyl? Did the historic Yaponchik have that much sway? Unbelievably, yes, he probably did. The real Yaponchik walked in and out of jails regularly with the assistance of several judges of the Supreme Court of the Russian Republic, and the approval of ranking politicians and social

CAN YOU PICTURE FRANK BLACK WITH AN EARRING?

CODE OF THE
VORY V ZAKONE[1]

1   A Thief must turn his back on his family, only the crime community is his family.
2   The Thief is forbidden to start a new family, no wives, no children.
3   The Thief is forbidden to work; his income must come only from criminal activity.
4   A Thief must give moral and material assistance to other Thieves using the 'obshchak', the communal money.
5   A Thief must give information about accomplices and their locations only in strict confidence.
6   If a Thief is under investigation, a petty thief must take responsibility on himself in order to allow the suspected Thief time to escape.
7   When a conflict arises in a crime family of Thieves, they cannot resolve it themselves. A meeting, a 'skhodka', of the *vor* will make the definitive decision.
8   Thieves must attend 'skhodka' when ordered, to provide a panel of peers to judge the Thief's conduct.
9   Punishment imposed by the 'skhodka' must be carried out.
10 A Thief must maintain his skills in the 'fenia', the Thieves' Jargon.
11 Thieves mustn't gamble unless they have the money to pay.
12 Thieves must recruit novices and train them.
13 A Thief must keep a 'shestiorka', a runner or gofer, in his 'employ'. Employ isn't actually a good translation, the 'shestiorka' serves the *vor*, but not usually for payment.
14 A Thief mustn't lose track of his tongue while drinking.
15 Thieves are forbidden any involvement with normal societal authorities. They can neither cooperate with nor claim help from, for example, the police.
16 Thieves do not participate in normal societal gatherings.
17 Thieves do not join social organizations.
18 Thieves do not bear weapons for the State, they do not serve in the army.
19 Thieves must fulfill any promise made to another Thief.

---

1 The Code presented here is an amalgam of several translations, not a word-by-word transcription, but, the sense of the Code remains intact.

CATCH IT? The number on the bottom of the helicopter that carried 'Yaponchik' to freedom was E-666 and, if you look closely, you'll see it repeated in Sergei's signature!

elitists. The Code of the Russian mob is the definitive answer to all *vor* questions, adhered to so tightly that the Russian Thieves make the Italian mafioso look like dilettantes, or children playing 'house'.

The theme throughout all the rules of the Code is simple: a thief doesn't accept society, he lives within a society of his own choosing, and within that society, he follows the rules. If that sounds remarkably like a cult, then the lengths to which a Thief will go for his superior starts to become evident. Russia is a country which has, for decades, attempted to crush anything it felt could threaten it, including the *Vory*, including the Church, and, especially, cults. Like most groups that've been forced underground, they tend to re-emerge even more tightly knit by the common experience than they were previously.

To the Thieves, a *Vor* demanded the same loyalty as a saint. Though there's no such rule in the Code, an oral tradition of acceptable and unacceptable conduct has arisen and, like the punishments under the Code itself, punishment for violating the unwritten rules is swift and usually lethal. When a *Vor* was approached on the street by 'freelancers', muggers with no criminal family, thieves who didn't 'profess the code', the *Vor* handed over his wallet and keys without a murmur. The following evening, his second returned the intact wallet, the car, and the heads of the two muggers. The devotion within the group is unquestioned. If the real Yaponchik had determined that something at Chernobyl was a threat to the group, and a 'skhodka' had supported that decision, then it's entirely possible that something would have gone wrong at Chernobyl. That the Chernobyl accident happened in the midst of a rising political revolution did nothing to dampen rumors that the accident was no accident, but, after many years of investigation, it's more likely the disaster was the result of stupidity than malice.

None of which would prevent the *Vor* from claiming an involvement if it increased the respect common citizens

afforded the Thieves as a whole. The risk of exposure as a fraud, while present, is almost negligible in a country where most of the citizens are primed to disbelieve government reports and where one in five schoolchildren, when asked what they wanted to be when they grew up, replied, 'Vor'!

Perhaps because so much of Russian life was carried out 'unofficially', everything from buying hamburgers to praying a matter to be hidden from the authorities, Russians seem primed to accept and encorporate myths and legends into their world view. Despite government denial of any religion, especially those that ended in a spectacular Armageddon, a number of apocalyptic cults did manage to arise in Russia and the former Soviet states.

In 1993, just outside Kiev, a young woman announced to her followers, the Great White Brotherhood, that she, Marian Tsvyguna, was the Messiah. Even after dressing in white robes that would have been quite fashionable in 'The Ten Commandments', carrying the crook-staff of an Egyptian king, and topping off her regalia with a Welsh witch's hat, Tsvyguna continued to attract followers. The presence of her husband, Krivonogov, who'd received training in psychological warfare before taking up a job as a youth counsellor, probably accounted for the increasing devotion of her closest followers. It was also a factor in explaining just why thousands of young people would begin slowly starving themselves to death in the belief that this would help their Maria Devi Christos, as Tsvyguna was now known, and 144,000 of her chosen people ascended to Heaven.

BLOOPER! Members of the Russian Orthodox Church cross themselves a little differently than Westerners do. Instead of head, heart, left, right, it's head, heart, right, left.

Luckily for the 'unchosen', Ukrainian authorities stepped in to squash the cult in November, before any of the seriously ill teens could die. In trying to understand how such a thing could develop so quickly, how a single woman could induce so many bright youngsters to follow her beyond the grave – especially when the scenario was clearly the other way around, Tsvyguna had absolutely no intention of dying

TESTIMONY TRIVIA 21

QUESTIONS

A single point for these easy ones!

1 What was found in the female victim's hair?
2 What was Yura's job in Chernobyl?
3 Where does 'Yaponchik' work?
4 What was the symbol found on the victim?
5 Where did Yura shoot 'Yaponchik'?

These will make you think.

6 What unusual load was in the handloaded shotgun shells?
7 What community did Brighton Beach remind the Russian immigrants of?
8 Which Biblical verse does Peter draw Frank's attention to?
9 What's a Zvezda?
10 What does Chernobyl mean in Ukrainian?

in the near future – they could only conclude that the area's troubled religious history had prepared her followers for a suicide attempt.

In fact, mass suicide is a recurring theme in Russian religious history. Between 1680 and 1730, some 20,000 able-minded Russians burned themselves to death in ritual suicides rather than submit to the government of the day's authority. Over 2,500 men, women and children would later immolate themselves inside a monastery in Paleostrovski in a bizarre Fire Baptism they believed would immediately deliver them from their physical misery into a spiritual haven. Outside present-day Vladivostok, fifteen nuns, convinced of the immediacy of the prophesied Second Coming, starved themselves to death rather than admit their predictions were wrong.

In an atmosphere where superstition, religion, loyalty and crime are so intrinsically intertwined, the Yaponchik of the Apocalypse wouldn't really be so terribly out of place.

NOTEBOOK:

Windows Into Faith

The Russian Orthodox Church, which officially didn't exist for half a century, is slowly reclaiming its churches, its treasures and its artisans. When the Communist regime made religion illegal and began turning churches into everything from office buildings to museums to morgues, an entire class of artists lost their livelihood. Sculptors, architects, iconographers, painters, and illuminators who'd been carefully maintaining the centuries old buildings were often imprisoned if they continued to produce religious art.

One such man, Igor Slaviskotov, is now eighty-three years old and, once again, creating the icons Russian Orthodoxy has seen as miniature chapels during the repression. He's finding it a very different world now. 'This triptych, a small thing really, for a family to keep in its home, was illegal just a few years ago. Now, not only is the church once more able to pay for this sort of work, but American tourists think of them as souvenirs, items they're willing to pay American dollars for.' His roommate is his brother, a gilder named Peter, who has even been approached by the larger art houses in New York. 'It's very popular there now, to have an icon made in the homeland. Many Russians live there, and, of course, there are non-Russian collectors who will pay big prices for anything big enough to be used as ordinary art.'

Peter would know. In order to raise the funds to get back to Russia from the small New York apartment where he and his family fled after Igor's arrest, Peter took on a commission for a smart interior design firm with a client who wanted an entire wall of his new home turned into a piece of iconoclastic art. The fee, $75,000 lets them

ANSWERS

These are the answers for the one pointers.

1 Gold leaf
2 Security Guard
3 The Consulate of the Russian Federation
4 The monogram of Christ
5 In the head

Two points for these.

6 Glass
7 Odessa
8 Revelations, 8:10
9 A brand of Russian cigarettes
10 Wormwood

YOUR SCORE:

all live comfortably while both men re-establish their connection with their boyhood church.

Will they be taking more commissions?

'No,' says Igor, 'The artist paints with his soul, for the Church, for God, for his family. I'm so busy with all the restoration that needs to be done, I've no time for outside commissions – and no desire for them either.'

HMMMMM? Though Peter Watts tells Frank that 'Chernobyl' means 'wormwood', the much more common translations are 'black grass' or 'black myth'.

INCIDENTALS:

'Maranatha', the title of this episode, comes from the Greek, 'Come, Our Lord'. Before deciding on this more obscure title, the episode had a much simpler title: 'The Second Coming'.

AND YOU THOUGHT YOUR MARRIAGE WAS STRESSFUL?!

CASE FILE: 'Paper Dove'

CASE SYNOPSIS:

Even on vacation, Frank Black can't escape his darker world. At the urging of Catherine's parents, he finds himself investigating the case of a family friend convicted of killing his wife. Frank's initial instinct, that the real killer remains free, turns shockingly solid when the killings continue and Catherine becomes a target.

KEY CITATION:

'He's silencing someone he knows, his wife or his mother. Once they're silenced, they become a captive audience. They'll still listen, be sympathetic, that's what he wants. That's why he never disfigures their faces.'

FRANK BLACK

VITAL STATISTICS:

Original US Airdate:	05/16/97
Production Number:	4C121
Written by:	Walon Green
	Ted Mann
Directed by:	Thomas Wright

Guest Cast:

Paul Raskin	The Figure
Mike Starr	Henry Dion
Linda Sorenson	Marie France Dion
Ken Pogue	Tom Miller
Maxine Miller	Justine Miller
Barbara Williams	Dawn
Michael St John Smith	Gil
Noah Dennis	Nick Scammel
Mitch Davies	Rich Scammel
Judy Norton	Carol Scammel
Eric Breker	Malcolm Hunziger
Doris Chilcott	Adele Hunziger
William Nunn	C R Hunziger
Arlene Jones	Agent Emmerlich
Todd Waite	Agent Kane
Frank Cassini	Agent Devlin
Garry Davey	Ranger Chet
Brenda McDonald	Mrs Steinbery
Angela Donahue	Amy Lee Walker

Death Toll:	1 female, throat destroyed
	1 female, stabbed and
	'garburated'

CASE HISTORY:

'CHEESE!' Click.

Click.

Click.

As Henry Dion and the mysterious man known only as The Figure happily snap away, creating little souvenirs of their odd vacations and preparing the next plain-manilla-envelope mailing for Frank Black, it's hard not to think of the number of killers who, anxious to 'record the moment', merely ended up giving the prosecution the star of their list of exhibits.

While killers have managed to convince juries that the murder weapon covered in their fingerprints, found in their trunk, and matched to the slugs taken from the victim wasn't

EVEN THE MILLERS' HOME ISN'T A RETREAT FOR FRANK BLACK

really theirs, not a single jury, when confronted with photographic evidence, has ever returned a 'not guilty' verdict!

Some, like Jeffrey Dahmer, who also shared Henry Dion's necrophilic tastes, would have done well to invest in Polaroid stock! One series of photos taken of a single body as Dahmer slowly reduced it to its component parts could have illustrated a formal text book on any or all of 'How to Butcher Your Own Game Animals', 'The D-I-Y Guide to Home Autopsies' or 'All You Wanted to Know About ... The Human Body'! Other photographs, apparently composed with an eye to their artistic merit and message, included a picture of a skeleton, bleached clear of any flesh, with its hands, feet and face left intact.

What purpose these images serve, for Dahmer or the hundreds of other killers who so carefully document their kills is rather uncertain. Some pictures evidently replace the 'trophies' other killers habitually keep, and they fulfill the same emotional function, mentally taking the killer back to those events to relive the high associated with the kill. Other killers, however, claim never to look at the pictures once they've been taken. Clemment Brady, who was convicted solely on the pictures found in his old army trunk, carried his camera everywhere, whether he was hunting for the young girls that turned him on, or just watching the local baseball team. His pictures of his victims, most of whom were crying or struggling to escape the bonds that really perked up Clemment's interest, left the jury in tears, but he claimed to have 'glanced at them as they were being developed' and then tossed them into the trunk because, 'Well, they're really not very good, you know, just didn't capture what I was going for.'

CATCH IT? What was the code the first victim used to arm her house alarm? 1013. That's also the name of the production company which makes *Millennium*. The company name came from the date 13 October, creator Chris Carter's birthday.

It probably didn't surprise anyone, Bentwood police included, when professional photographer/killer Gerald Brill's scrapbook included studio quality photos of nearly four years' worth of rape victims. He might never have been caught if not for an observant young officer finding something vaguely familiar in a photo that appeared on the cover of an underground magazine confiscated in a raid. Not only

had Brill raped, beaten, and subjected his victims to the indignity of posing for his bizarre gratification, he'd sold the photos for profit! The jury was not kind.

    Killer couples have gotten in on the photography act too, not only photographing their unusually aberrant couplings, but whatever indignities they could heap on their joint victims. Bernardo and Hmolka, the Canadian couple who sexually assaulted and murdered a number of young women, including Hmolka's younger sister, recorded their escapades in living color and sound. So did Ian Brady and Myra Hindley, the Moors Murderers. Their audiotape of a ten-year-old child begging for her life so horrified the court that veteran police officers cried.

    The advances in technology made even the clumsiest of serial rapists and murderers into overnight impresarios capable of near-professional sophistication when it came to creating their mementos. Videotape became nearly as common as photographic evidence and, with the addition of motion and

WILL FRANK STILL BE SMILING WHEN HE RETURNS TO THE JEEP IN THE SECOND SEASON PREMIÈRE?

TESTIMONY TRIVIA 22

QUESTIONS

The easy ones.

1 What's Catherine's maiden name?
2 What's the bedtime treat in Catherine's family home?
3 What did Dion sing to Amy Lee Walker?
4 Which agent did Henry call at the FBI?
5 With what kitchen utensil did Mrs Dion threaten Henry?

The not-so-easy ones.

6 What language has Catherine been teaching Jordan?
7 To what mythical figure did Dion compare Amy?
8 To what museum did Catherine take Jordan?
9 Where does Henry Dion take a corpse 'camping'?
10 What did Mrs Hunziger give Jordan?

sound, leaving even less to the jury's imagination, the perpetrator's chances of getting off plummeted. Clarence Milton knew there was videotape of him killing his brother's wife, after all, he'd taken the film, but, because his face was covered during his appearances on tape, he felt sure it could never be used to convict him. He wasn't much of a student of history.

Jerome Henry, who preferred the simple Polaroid camera, had been equally sure he couldn't be connected with the pictures he'd taken of a corpse dressed in his wide collection of shoes. He didn't realize he'd also captured his smiling reflection in an on-camera piece of glass. Clarence Milton's reflection turned up in the high-gloss finish of a canoe!

BLOOPER! Whatever agency Henry Dion worked for needed a geography lesson. According to the number Henry wrote down, 212-555-0163, they sent him all the way to New York City for a single shift! Not much profit in that.

Not all murdering photographers share the same prioritization scheme; for some, the pictures themselves are the objects of desire, the bodies used to create the pictures hardly separable from the other props required to produce the deathly tableaux. Henri Nadeau was one such killer. A failed painter, a failed

musician, and a failed actor, Henri seemed blessed with creative impulses, but absolutely no talent – until he discovered
slash art in some pulp magazines. Suddenly, his fascination
with death, his part-time job at the morgue, and his thwarted
artistic impulses crashed together in a mind already some-
what deficient in the moral and ethical categories. At first,
he simply snuck his camera into the mortu-
ary, quickly posed the bodies there, clicked
away, and then put everything back the way
he'd found it. While his tastes weren't
exactly mainstream, up to that point, he
hadn't actually committed a crime. It was
when he decided the reason his own efforts
at slash art weren't up to 'snuff' and blamed
it on the stale nature of the corpses available to him that he began sliding into the
realm of the criminally insane.

HMMMMM? There's a rather dilapidated flag hanging under glass as a decoration in the Hunziger's Virginia home, a rather fitting piece in an area which prides itself on its Civil War history. There's just one problem with this particular flag. Though it's in terrible shape, there are at least 46 stars on it! There's no way it could be a Civil War heirloom!

His first kill was a young woman
who'd partied too heartily and decided to
sleep it off in her car rather than drive home.
He described the experience succinctly.
'Quick. I did it quickly. I didn't want to hurt her, just kill her.'
If the statements of her friends are accurate, Henri was lucky
not to be caught his first time out. A girlfriend inside had
decided to run the victim home and was the first to discover
blood, but no girl, inside the car. Henri, with beginner's luck,
had struck in the few moments it took for her friend to
change into a warm sweater, tie up her shoes and find her
purse.

Oblivious to his close call, Henri's biggest problem was
the blood that would horrify her friend. The unplanned
killing had left Henri with few options for actually killing his
victim. His weapon, a pocketknife more suited to trimming
cigars, had left the girl's throat a mangled mess. The resultant
photos were, in Henri's opinion, 'spoiled' because of the limitations set on him by her horrid throat wound. 'I could only
work in three-quarter view.'

He was ready next time and left his second victim, a
young co-ed walking home alone, almost unmarred by strangling her with a silk scarf. 'The bruising was easy to cover

with body paint.' More satisfied with these efforts, he was anxious to continue and killed three more women in quick succession. Still, despite racking up a total of five victims, Henri Nadeau isn't really considered a serial killer. He fails to conform to the unspoken rule that serial killings must be sexually motivated. Henri neither raped not lusted after his victims, they were props, nothing more. On a rather morbid sidenote, his photos, which were reprinted after his trial, were, for a short time, in high demand. He'd apparently discovered his niche.

NOTEBOOK:

GUEST FILMOGRAPHY:
MIKE STARR

EZ Streets (1996) – Mickey Kinnear
Blood and Wine (1996) – Mike
James and the Giant Peach (1996) – Beat Cop
Just Your Luck (1996) – Veteran Cop
Two If By Sea (1996) – Fitzie
3rd Rock from the Sun (1996) – Aggravated Neighbor
High Incident (1996) – Assault Suspect
Clockers (1995) – Thumper
A Pyromaniac's Love Story (1995) – Sergeant Zikowski
News Radio (1995) – Building Super
Nowhere Man (1995) – Bert Williams
Hardball (1994) – Mike Widmer

Cabin Boy (1994) – Mulligan

Dumb & Dumber (1994) – Joe Mentalino

Ed Wood (1994) – Georgie Weiss

The Hudsucker Proxy (1994) – Newsroom Reporter

On Deadly Ground (1994) – Big Mike

Trial By Jury (1994) – Hughie Bonner

Mad Dog and Glory (1993) – Harold

Night Trap (1993) – Detective Williams

Son of the Pink Panther (1993) – Hanif

The Bodyguard (1992) – Tony

Freejack (1992) – Shaggy Man

Mac (1992) – Fireman

Me and Veronica (1992) – Vinnie

Billy Bathgate (1991) – Julie Martin

Blue Steel (1990) – Superintendant

GoodFellas (1990) – Frenchy

Miller's Crossing (1990) – Frankie

Shock to the System (1990) – Bum 3

Born on the Fourth of July (1989) – Man

The Chair (1989) – Wilson

Kojak: Ariana (1989) – Hamilton

Lean On Me (1989) – Mr Zirella

Funny Farm (1988) – Crocker

The Money Pit (1986) – Lenny

Off Beat (1986) – James Bonnell

Cat's Eye (1985) – Ducky

The Last Dragon (1985) – Rock

▶ ▶ ▶ ▶ ▶ ▶

THE TESTIMONY TRIVIA SCORECARD

Okay, this is Volume Two so no gimme points just for playing. This time you've got to earn them! See if your observational skills have improved since the last time you peered into the world of Frank Black.

00–24:   You're joking right? I mean, I'm just so surprised you could even find the second page of the application. Look, let's be straight up here. If you were the last investigator on the face of the planet, we still wouldn't hire you. We might be covert, but we still have standards, ya know.

25–49:   Sorry, bud, but you're still strictly a wanna-be. Maybe you should try heading off to a remote motel for a 5 May, 2000, vacation? I seem to recall hearing about some sort of wanna-be convention for around that time. Maybe you could start your own group, the 500 Group perhaps?

50–75:   You know, there's real potential here, something the Group could work with. Of course, there are other tests to pass first. Okay, have you ever been remanded to a mental institution for 'seeing things differently?' Hey, don't worry, that's not necessarily an obstacle to career advancement ...

76–100+:   You say you can't seem to forget the details of any case you've ever worked? Really? And you're wondering if there really is a common thread here or if you're just being paranoid. Well, you know what they say, 'Just because everyone's out to get you doesn't make you paranoid.' Let's talk.

PHOTOGRAPHIC ACKNOWLEDGEMENTS

Grateful acknowledgement is made for permission to reprint the following photographs:

Pages 67, 95, 108 © Fox Broadcasting/courtesy of Photofest

Page 100 © Tri-Star Pictures/courtesy of Photofest

Pages 88, 90 © Marcel Indik/ Outline

Pages 20, 53 © Stephen Danelian/Outline

Pages 52, 63 © Tony Costa/Outline

Pages 59, 121 © Steve Labadessa/Outline

Pages 31, 71 © Courtesy Everett Collection

Page 11 © 20th Century Fox Film Corp./courtesy Everett Collection

All other photos: © Fox Broadcasting/courtesy Everett Collection

ABOUT THE AUTHOR

N. E. GENGE lives and works out of the far reaches of northern Canada. She is a documentary scriptwriter as well as the author of two historical biographies, and a regular contributor to publications such as *The Times*. Her fiction has appeared in *Aboriginal Science Fiction, Asimov's Science Fiction* and *Story*. As the author of *The Unofficial X-Files Companion, The New Unofficial X-Files Companion* and *The Unofficial Millennium Companion Volume One*, she is something of an expert on Chris Carter's creations.

THE UNOFFICIAL

Millennium
Companion

THE COVERT CASEBOOK
OF THE
MILLENNIUM GROUP

VOLUME ONE

The successor to *The X-Files* is here ...

Frank Black works for the Millennium Group, a mysterious and totally covert organization controlled by the FBI, and Agent Black has talents which the FBI desperately needs...

For those whose curiosity about the future harbors a darker side, *The Unofficial Millennium Companion* provides a compelling look into Chris Carter's latest creation. The first behind-the-scenes companion to the series, the book includes:

- interviews with members of the real-life Academy Group – the mysterious organization that inspired Chris Carter to create the Millennium Group
- background details on the FBI, its operatives and their targets
- a crash course in 'millennial thinking', covering the prophecies, portents and predictions of such famous futurists as Nostradamus and Isaac Asimov, both of whom have influenced *Millennium*'s riveting backdrop
- background information on the real-life events threaded through every episode
- photos of the Millennium Group's travels

'*Millennium* is dark, sick sin filmed with consummate class. It's like *Seven* to the power of seven, with added steals from *The Silence of the Lambs*' *The Guardian*